Discovering
God's
Will

Also by Troy Fitzgerald

ChristWise: Discipleship Guide for Juniors

ChristWise: Discipleship Guide for Teens

ChristWise: Discipleship Guide for Youth

ChristWise: Leader's Guide for Juniors, Teens, and Youth

Forty Days Wild: Training Camp for Spiritual Growth

Out of the Shipyard: Launching an Effective Youth Ministry

A practical guide to

Discovering
God's
Will

Troy Fitzgerald

Pacific Press® Publishing Association
Nampa, Idaho
Oshawa, Ontario, Canada
www.pacificpress.com

Cover design by Michelle C. Petz
Inside design by Steve Lanto
Cover photo © iStockphoto.com

ISBN 13: 978-0-8163-2180-3
ISBN 10: 0–8163–2180-9

Additional copies of this book are available by calling toll-free 1-800-765-
6955 or by visiting http://www.adventistbookcenter.com.

07 08 09 10 11 • 5 4 3 2 1

Dedicated . . .

to my parents, Don and Helen Fitzgerald,
for the way you hang on to God's hand in the ups and downs
and hear His voice in the noise and in the silence.

Special thanks . . .

to Tim Lale and the rest of the Pacific Press team,
who patiently and faithfully produce inspiring reading material.

to the young people in my youth group who have grown up right
before my very eyes.
You have taught me many things about discovering God's will.
You are my champions of the journey!

to Karl Haffner, my dear friend and mentor.
You are the Mehahsheerah of the fairway!

to Leslie, Henning, John, and Debbie,
my pastoral teammates at the College Church.
Your devotion and the way you live and serve
has blessed my growth and my family unmistakably.

to John Loor Jr., Jerry Nelson, Curtis Wright,
Craig Heinrich, and Ken Rogers
for giving me the opportunities to serve!
You have marked my life in so many good ways.

to my lovely bride, Julia, and my precious boys, Cameron and Morgan—
you are my joy!

Contents

Core
Beliefs

I'm curious about the questions that burn in people. I'm equally sensitive—maybe oversensitive—to what people don't care about as well; call it insecurity, or chalk it up to something missing in my childhood. The point is, I can't stomach the thought of writing about stuff that others think is meaningless. But if there is one question that stirs inside both believers and seekers, it's the issue of discovering God's will. Over and over again, I hear people ask, "What does God want from me, and how will He reveal His plan for my life?"

Rarely are people "preoccupied" with any one topic, so, to suggest that everyone is "thinking" or "asking" a certain question about "only one thing" is somewhat dubious. However, when I've raised the topic of "knowing God's will," I've found that people are eager to hear about it. The Barna Research Group discovered that nearly two-thirds of Americans were facing decisions about which they wanted some direction from God.[1] My personal experience confirms the depths of the desire to know what God wants with our lives.

The topic is especially pressing for young adults because they make most of their long-term decisions in the span of a few stressful years. Here are a few of the questions about God's will that I've collected from students:

- "What does God want from me?"
- "Why does God make it so hard [for us] to know Him?"

- "Does the Bible tell me everything I need to know to make good decisions?"
- "Does God have a specific plan for my life, or is it up to me?"
- "Will doing God's will make me happy, successful, and secure?"
- "How do I determine what God wants me to become?"
- "How will I know that God's will for me is His will and not my own?"
- "How does God reveal His will to me?"
- "Will my bad choices in the past disqualify me from knowing and living God's will now and in the future?"
- "Why doesn't God answer my prayer for direction in life when others get swinging doors that open and shut, not to mention fully functioning windows when the doors aren't working?"

And my all-time favorite . . .

- "What ever happened to the Urim and Thummin, that 'Yes' or 'No' jacket the priests used in the old days? I could use one of those about now (in a neutral color, of course)."

However, discovering God's will is not only a quest for young adults. It matters to anyone seeking God's input on major decisions. Coming to an understanding of how He guides is just as important to those who are, let's say, young at heart as it is to those who actually are young. At every stage of life, we make pivotal decisions. So, if God has something to say, most people I know want to hear it.

When I began to speak on the topic of God's will for our life, people swooped down from nowhere to join the fray. The flood of comments and questions made it clear that the imprecise language and the barrage of obtuse clichés about God's guidance we frequently hear have made some of the issues unintelligible. So, before we begin this journey, I must tip my hand as to the core beliefs I hold about discovering and living God's will.

Core belief #1: There must be a will . . . and therefore a way.

Jesus stated, " 'Enter through the narrow gate. For wide is the gate and broad is the road that leads to destruction, and many enter through it. But small is the gate and narrow the road that leads to life, and only a few find it' " (Matthew 7:13). Isaiah promised, "Whether you turn to the right or to the left, your ears will hear a voice behind you, saying, 'This is the way; walk in it' " (Isaiah 30:21). David sang to God,

> You have made known to me the path of life;
>   you will fill me with joy in your presence,
>   with eternal pleasures at your right hand (Psalm 16:11).

And the wise guy who wrote the book of Proverbs warned us to be careful of our own wisdom, claiming, "There is a way that seems right to a man, / but in the end it leads to death" (Proverbs 14:12). Clearly, if there is a will, then there must be a way.

The prophet Jeremiah affirmed this, saying,

> This is what the LORD says:
> "Stand at the crossroads and look;
>   ask for the ancient paths,
> ask where *the good way is*, and *walk in it*,
>   and you will find rest for your souls" (Jeremiah 6:16; emphasis added).

However, that verse in Jeremiah's book contains one more line: "But you said, 'We will not walk in it.' " Ultimately, the path we walk is our choice to make.

There are many examples of individuals whose lives seem to march across the landscape on a divine path. As I consider the storied lives of people who have chosen to follow God, I've found it increasingly believable that there is a God who has a will and a way to live.

Core belief #2: God has communicated His will in a way that we can understand and know how to follow.

Communication with God is the tipping point in our relationship with Him. I have a friend with whom I communicate regularly. While our interaction may be regular, it is anything but normal. I send him e-mails, and he writes me with pen, ink, and stamp. I don't understand this phenomenon—he has e-mail! (He's one of those e-mail joke "forwarders.") One time I received a note from him enclosed in a motion-sickness bag from the airplane he was on. He's weird and even a bit eccentric, but he replies to me; I'm just not certain of the method by which he'll choose to communicate. I'm waiting for the day I see a small plane flying over my house trailing white smoke that says, "Hey Troy, got your e-mail. Do you wanna golf tomorrow?" The trick will be knowing when to look up in the sky.

What do you expect to see or hear when you ask God to "show me Your will"? A dream? A feeling? A sign? How will you interpret a seeming "no answer"? In what form do you think the answer will come? Our expectations about God's guidance have everything to do with communication actually taking place. If we are expecting guidance, it won't escape us.

God hasn't abandoned us to guessing games or left us with only cryptic riddles as to the way through the darkness. He's a communicator par excellence! But communication is effective only if both parties pay attention. This leaves us with the task of looking at God's chosen communication process—from *how* He communicates to *what* He communicates. The promise remains for everyone: " 'You will seek me and find me when you seek me with all your heart' " (Jeremiah 29:13).

You will discover God's will for your life as a result of deliberate seeking and courageous living. It doesn't just happen. You must value God's will more than anything else. In a way, the journey will cost you everything. But if you believe that the plans God has for you are better than your own, seek God with all your heart. And remember, God is more persistent and more creative than you or I will ever be. Ray Pritchard said, "God wants you to know His will more than you want to know it, and therefore He takes personal responsibility to see that you discover it."[2] Communication involves a conversation in which two parties are listening. While God takes the initiative in starting the communication process, there will be work for you in discovering and doing His will.

Core belief #3: Knowing God's will for our lives is more about knowing God than about knowing the future.

Getting guidance from God rarely involves a vision of the future; it's more a matter of having a relationship with God in the present. While searching for a place called Chain Lakes just outside of Yosemite National Park, I got lost on the logging roads. I pulled over to the side of the dusty road I was on to ask directions from a man who was securing the logs on his truck. I inquired, "Am I on the right road to get to Chain Lakes, or is there another road?"

He smirked and snorted and said, "You can't get there from here."

I couldn't believe he actually said that. Obviously, this guy watched too much TV. In my mind, a person should be able to get to anywhere from anywhere. After all, this is America.

I waited until it was clear that he didn't intend to unpack his prophetic maxim. Then I pressed him to elaborate. "Why? How can you say that?"

He replied, "You can get to Chain Lakes only by hiking or horseback, young man."

He was right. Neither the road I was on nor any other road on that mountain would take me to the place called Chain Lakes. I would have to take a walk—a five-mile hike through the mountains—to get there.

This principle applies to so many aspects of living. Strong marriages don't happen accidentally. Good grades don't find their way onto a transcript unless you study and do the work. You can't become skilled in sports without training, no matter how athletic you might be. Playing the cello requires practice. Saving money happens when you choose to go without something you want. Shortcuts and the easy way don't exist on this journey. As the guy said, "You can't get there from here." The narrow way referred to earlier is a walk—a hike—a hand-to-hand journey with Jesus Himself. There is no other way. If you want guidance without the Guide, seek out the wisdom waiting for you in the center of a fortune cookie. Knowing God's will is more about knowing God than about knowing exactly what to do at every crossroad in your life.

Thinking about giving up?

Not only does the Bible convey that there is a will for us to live, but I feel the truth of this idea intuitively. I think one of the crazy paradoxes of the postmodern world is that our experience is supposed to be the source of authority for what is real and right. But we've learned that trusting only in our experience may not be wise. Perhaps our experience has let us down when it comes to believing that God is good. Unanswered prayers. Tragedy. Silence. Obstacles. Loneliness. Mean people. Cancer. Abuse. Alienation. If our experience alone determines what we think is true, then I can't imagine how some could even choke out a prayer to God.

Here's something that is only a theory—but think about it: I believe most people struggle more with questions about who God is and what He's like than with whether or not He exists. If God is so good, why do so many bad things happen? If God is in control, why does evil reign? If God is so close and loving, why do I feel as if there's a Grand Canyon between us? In moments of disaster, unbelievers will often shake their fists at a God they don't believe in. They stew in anger at the Something or Someone who should have prevented the disaster.

Sometimes God's quietness can steal the hope from the strongest seeker. A personal relationship with God can sour quickly when we seek but don't find. The whole experience of intimacy with God seems far too unreal and unattainable. Unfortunately, it is common for us to receive a busy signal when seeking His guidance in our lives. For some, the lack of an answer quickly rouses a resounding "I don't care" or "I'm not interested" or "I don't have time for this," and we dismiss God from the equation of our lives because "obviously" He has dismissed us from His.

People hate being ignored more than they hate being hated. To hate requires an emotional commitment toward the other person. To be indifferent administers the ultimate slap in the face, virtually saying, "You don't matter." I'm guessing that some feel like they don't matter to God because the Almighty doesn't return their calls. No direction. No guidance. But I testify that God has not been silent. He is anything but indifferent. God has been trying harder to get to us than any one of us has ever sought Him. It may even be that He is more preoccupied with our future than we are. The essence of God's interaction with humanity is to guide us into a meaningful relationship with Him. But the message can get lost if we aren't looking in the right places.

Discovering God's Will doesn't attempt to provide magical formulas for choosing the right college or tips to get God to tell you whom you should marry. While I am being forthright about the beliefs that underpin this book, I am also keenly aware of how many unanswered questions I have about God's guiding ways. If I am certain about anything, it is that I am a child on a journey. In many ways, this book is a conversation. While it sounds part story, part sermon, and part personal struggle, I'm hoping that you can interact with the ideas in such a way that it is helpful for you. My prayer is that this conversation can remove some misconceptions about God's guidance and deepen our commitment to live each day in step with the Savior.

Count on it: There is a God who cares, and He is prepared to answer a few of our questions. There is a God who deeply feels our emptiness, and He longs to fill us with meaning and purpose. There is a God who claims to be able to give us perspective in our confusion and comfort in our pain. There is a God who will make good on all His promises. God knows us and seeks us. Actually, He comes right out with it: " 'I know the plans I have for you,' declares the LORD, 'plans to prosper you and not to harm you, plans to give you hope and a future. Then you will call upon me and come and pray to me, and I will listen to you. You will seek me and find me when you seek me with all your heart' " (Jeremiah 29:11–13).

With all my heart, I believe God has a will for us to live. I believe it is possible to know His will for our life. And I believe walking confidently in God's will is well within reach of every believer.

---

1. Robert Jeffress, *Hearing the Master's Voice: The Comfort and Confidence of Knowing God's Will* (Colorado Springs, Colo.: WaterBrook Press, 2001), 17.

2. Ray Pritchard, *The Road Best Traveled: Knowing God's Will for Your Life* (Wheaton, Ill.: Crossway Books, 1995), 18.

Part I

The Search
for God's Will

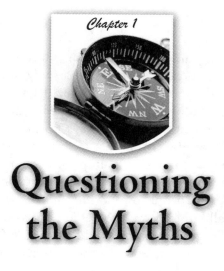

Chapter 1

Questioning the Myths

Once you miss the first buttonhole, you never manage to button up right.

Growing up, I rarely wore shirts that had to be buttoned because I'd become frustrated when I found I'd buttoned my shirt crookedly. I'd started by putting the wrong button in the buttonhole. This is why I'm a T-shirt guy. But the principle of starting by making all the right adjustments is one we should apply to finding God's will. We'll make one of those "adjustments" by checking our assumptions about the way God reveals His will to people.

Assumptions are tricky. They shape the way we view the world around us. Sometimes, if our assumptions are faulty, unbalanced, or uninformed, we think things that simply don't work. And we may even defend completely irrational ideas.

Consider the television show *Candid Camera*. The purpose of the show is to get random people to do absolutely ridiculous things—captured for our viewing pleasure by a hidden camera. The show is hilarious because the actors get participants to do the most ridiculous things but treat the behavior in a way that compels the participants to mindlessly embrace their actions as normal.

For example, they might ask someone walking down a busy street to honk an antique bike horn (the kind that clowns use) every time someone else walks by without looking at the participant. Amazingly, the show's personnel actually find people willing to do it. And every time an unsuspecting passerby doesn't make eye contact with the horn-blower, the obnoxious noise scares them into eye contact—and sometimes into an energized conversation. Even more amazingly, the more irrationally the dupes behave, the more vigorously they defend their behavior. Essentially, the abnormal becomes normal simply out of mindless repetition. This illustrates that there are always unspoken assumptions that guide (or misguide) our behavior.

Whether we like it or not, our assumptions about what is normal and expected frame how we perceive God communicating His will to people. And much like the people on *Candid Camera*, as life becomes complicated, we find all kinds of ways to defend our assumptions about the way God works. So, the first step to understanding God's will better is to be clear about our assumptions on the matter. Without a thoughtful check on our own preconceptions, we might base our beliefs about God's guidance on happenstance—like the puppy mentioned in the following story:

A couple brought a puppy home and let him play in the backyard. The puppy saw a baby squirrel in a tree and ran over to the base of the tree, sat down, and began to bark. The barking scared the baby squirrel, so it tried to jump to another branch farther away. But the poor squirrel missed his jump and fell straight into the open mouth of the puppy. Then, for the next fifteen years, the dog sat at the base of that tree and barked, waiting for another squirrel to fall from the sky into his open jaws.

As we look at some of the myths that grow out of our assumptions about God's will, it is important to note that each myth has at least a kernel of truth to it. If we were to bank our expectation of discovering God's plan for our life all on one approach, we would be like the dog under the tree waiting for a squirrel to drop miraculously into his mouth. Examine the following myths, and consider what you know about God's guidance, leaving room for what you don't know.

Myth #1: God's will is a mystery we need to solve.

When I was in college, a church member slipped a hundred bucks in a card and mailed it to me anonymously. Well, *almost* anonymously. During church, he asked from the pulpit if there was anything we wanted to thank God for this week, and then he peered intently at me. At first I was thankful, but the more he stared at me, the more uncomfortably suspicious I became. He continued to juggle praise from the congregation and to look at me as if I were going to pop with gratefulness at any moment. I was so embarrassed that I wanted to crawl under the pew. It was as if he were trying desperately to keep a secret and shout it to the world at the same time.

Some contend that God knows the secret about His plan for our life, but He's not allowed to tell. They think that it is up to us to discover His plan by figuring it out from a few cryptic hints sent from heaven. I don't think so. God is unmistakably clear about what He knows and what He tells people:

> "For I know the plans I have for you," declares the LORD, "plans to prosper you and not to harm you, plans to give you hope and a future" (Jeremiah 29:11).

> "I make known the end from the beginning,
> from ancient times, what is still to come.
> I say: My purpose will stand,
> and I will do all that I please" (Isaiah 46:10).

> There is surely a future hope for you,
> and your hope will not be cut off (Proverbs 23:18).

> "So there is hope for your future," declares the LORD.
> "Your children will return to their own land" (Jeremiah 31:17).

> But the plans of the LORD stand firm forever,
> the purposes of his heart through all generations (Psalm 33:11).

I don't see God's plan as a puzzle. He has a plan, and it will come to pass. He has a will for your life, and He declares it, conveys it, commands it, and reveals it freely to those who are eager to know it.

I struggle to see 3-D pictures. Others stare into them, and the image emerges rather clearly and without much drama. Not me. I squint, blink, search, scan, imagine, and peer into those pictures with all I've got, but I can never see the image within the speckles.

A fourth-grader took it upon himself to educate me about 3-D pictures, and, behold, my eyes were opened! The first trick he showed me was to start by reading the instructions. It is amazing how much valuable information clearly marked instructions contain. The next trick was to stare patiently into the picture. I hadn't been looking at the picture continuously, waiting for the hidden image to emerge. Sure enough, the little rascal of a fourth-grader succeeded in coaching me to see the image clearly.

Is knowing God's will like knowing the secret to seeing the hidden image in 3-D pictures? Does God conceal Himself beyond the apparent reality, playing hide-and-seek with humanity? According to Scripture, God has made His will known to the world by His Word and through His Son. Listen to what the writer of Hebrews said: "In the past God spoke to our forefathers through the prophets at many times and in various ways, but in these last days he has spoken to us by his Son, whom he appointed heir of all things, and through whom he made the universe. The Son is the radiance of God's glory and the exact representation of his being, sustaining all things by his powerful word" (Hebrews 1:1–3).

I don't think God is playing with our life as though His will were a riddle to be solved or a puzzle to be put together. Although discovering His will involves searching, we are not seeking out a God who is hiding.

Myth #2: God has a very specific plan for our lives.

"What if this is *the one*?" Carly pleaded.

"Which one?" I replied.

Apparently, Carly's boyfriend was moving to another college, and she had to decide whether to transfer with him or to break up and remain at home. She loved him—this was evident. But her current dilemma confused her, and she was hoping God would have some direction for her.

"Do you mean *the only one*?" I pressed.

"Doesn't God have the perfect match out there for us? I mean, I'm sure there is more than one person I *could* marry, but is there one person I *should* marry?"

Is there some perfect master plan in heaven that would enable us, if we were to make just the right choices, to experience blissful living? Is God's plan for our life a chess match in which every decision determines the destiny of the player?

That notion seems absurd. If God's will is one specific life scenario or a projected master plan of minute, detailed experiences, then what happens when I make one bad choice? Am I out of the plan? Do I descend to an inferior track of life where my potential might be OK but not as good as it would have been had I chosen better? Do I go from plan A to plan B to plan C and so on? If God's will for me is a story already written that simply requires matching the right choices with the right situation, how do we know how and when to choose appropriately? What happens if I make a mistake? What happens if I have a bad day?

J. I. Packer maintains that the idea that God has a specific, detailed plan for our life is a misconception analogous to traveling with an itinerary drawn up by a travel agent: "As long as you are in the right place at the right time to board each plane or train or bus or boat, all is well. But miss one of the preplanned connections, and the itinerary is ruined. A revised plan can only ever be second-best compared with the original."[1]

If this myth is prominent today, it is no wonder that frustration and unrest cripple people. Everything depends on discovering God's specific path for you. If figuring out how to discover that Mount Everest–sized morsel of information were not enough to worry you, what about the fact that you still have to make the right choice, not just sometimes or once in a while, but always. Initially, this idea of a prepackaged plan might sound comforting, but follow this branch out from the tree trunk, and it's just downright bad for your health.

Jerry Sittser likens this model of understanding God's will to a maze: "In this model, then, when a decision has to be made, life suddenly becomes like a maze. There is only one way out. All the other ways are dead ends, every one of them a bad choice. . . . If we choose rightly, we will experience his blessing and achieve success and happiness. If we choose wrongly, we may lose our way and miss God's will for our lives and remain lost forever in an incomprehensible maze."[2]

Again, when you ask people to question the assumption that an all-knowing and loving God would wire up one ideal plan for us to discover and choose, the folly of such a plan eventually emerges. One of the most basic concepts we must get before digging too deeply into His plan is that God can be all-knowing all the time, yet be completely free to let humans choose as they please. The fact that God knows doesn't mean that God chooses or determines a course for us. I don't want to meander down the path of thinking that I know what God knows and doesn't know. Some theologians—although I think well intentioned—have sought to determine what God knows and what He is incapable of knowing based on what they conceive. The problem is obvious: God's knowledge, power, and abilities are well beyond the limits of our understanding:

> "My thoughts are not your thoughts,
> neither are your ways my ways," declares the LORD.

"As the heavens are higher than the earth,
　　so are my ways higher than your ways
　　and my thoughts than your thoughts" (Isaiah 55:8, 9).

The problem is not what God knows or doesn't know. It's how limited we are as finite beings to comprehend it. I don't know how much God knows, and I'm not sure I want to be the one to try to delineate it—simply because I have a hard time understanding it.

It is true that God does declare ahead of time aspects of a person's destiny. He told Abraham to go and become the great-grandfather of the One who would save the world:

"I will make you into a great nation
　　and I will bless you;
I will make your name great,
　　and you will be a blessing" (Genesis 12:2).

Moses was saved miraculously in a basket and brought up with the training of a king to prepare him to lead God's people out of slavery and into the Promised Land. There is no question that Moses was hand-picked at birth for a specific purpose in life. After Moses had been prepared by the wilderness, God said, " 'I have indeed seen the misery of my people in Egypt. . . . I am sending you to Pharaoh to bring my people the Israelites out of Egypt' " (Exodus 3:7, 10).

As the need for a new king arose in Israel, God had one man in mind: " 'Fill your horn with oil and be on your way; I am sending you to Jesse of Bethlehem. I have chosen one of his sons to be king' " (1 Samuel 16:1). After Samuel looked over all the brothers, young David was brought in before the prophet, and the Lord said to Samuel, " 'Rise and anoint him; he is the one' " (verse 12).

Esther, a woman whose life is characterized by one special moment of courage, was the right person in the right place at the right time: " 'If you remain silent at this time, relief and deliverance for the Jews will arise from another place, but you and your father's family will perish. And who knows but that you have come to royal position for such a time as this?' " (Esther 4:14).

Even before John the Baptist was conceived, he had a specific destiny. The particulars of his life were clear in God's mind right down to his gender, name, dietary habits, and most of all, his mission in life:

"Your wife Elizabeth will bear you a son, and you are to give him the name John. He will be a joy and delight to you, and many will rejoice because of his birth, for he will be great in the sight of the Lord. He is never to take wine or other fermented drink, and he will be filled with the Holy Spirit even from birth. Many of the people of Israel will he bring back to the Lord their God. And he will go on before the Lord, in the spirit and power of Elijah, to turn the hearts of the fathers to their children and the disobedient to the wisdom of the righteous—to make ready a people prepared for the Lord" (Luke 1:13–17).

Special people? Yes! Born with a specific destiny? It seems so. But if the psalmist speaks for all of us, then what is true for John, Esther, Moses, and Abe is true for you and me.

You created my inmost being;
    you knit me together in my mother's womb.
I praise you because I am fearfully and wonderfully made;
    your works are wonderful,
    I know that full well.
My frame was not hidden from you
    when I was made in the secret place.
When I was woven together in the depths of the earth,
    your eyes saw my unformed body.
All the days ordained for me
    were written in your book
    before one of them came to be.

How precious to me are your thoughts, O God!
    How vast is the sum of them! (Psalm 139:13–17).

You remember David, the chosen king of Israel? If our decisions make and break whether or not we are in the specific plan of God, how can the following be said about David, who became a willful adulterer and a murderer: " 'After He had removed him, He raised up David to be their king, concerning whom He also testified and said, "*I HAVE FOUND DAVID* the son of Jesse, *A MAN AFTER MY HEART*, who *will do all My will*" ' " (Acts 13:22, NASB; emphasis added). Surely, that little issue with Bathsheba and Uriah hadn't been written into the grand scheme of things. Yet the book of Acts records David as a man who did "all" God's will.

Surely a theologically moderate theologian like Paul would have a more realistic spin on the specific nature of God's will. But he wrote, "Praise be to the God and Father of our Lord Jesus Christ, who has blessed us in the heavenly realms with every spiritual blessing in Christ. For he chose us in him before the creation of the world to be holy and blameless in his sight. In love he predestined us to be adopted as his sons through Jesus Christ, in accordance with his pleasure and will—to the praise of his glorious grace, which he has freely given us in the One he loves" (Ephesians 1:3–6).

From our perspective, Abraham, Moses, and David all made choices that should have stymied God's grand design. Abraham forfeited his bride when times got tough. Moses lost his temper when tensions were high. David stole another man's wife after sneaking a peek on the rooftops.

Does God's will change as a result of our decisions? All decisions do have consequences. To what degree did their decisions—do our decisions—affect God's ultimate goal? This is what we know:

- God has a plan for every individual.
- God works in all manner of ways to see His plan through.
- God's plan allows people to choose freely.
- Our choices don't necessarily change God's plan—only our position in reference to His ultimate goal. (If I choose to live outside or completely away from God's will, His ultimate purpose is not thwarted; see Job 42:1, 2.)

Since God will not allow His ultimate purpose to be thwarted, He guides in a number of ways, and His methods of revealing His will often change. Consider the methods through which God chose to guide people:

- The sanctuary in the desert
- A cloud and a pillar of fire
- Balaam's donkey
- A trumpet blast
- A jeweled vest worn by the high priest
- A flood of water

- The absence of water
- Fire from heaven
- A still, small voice on a mountain
- Parted waters, impossible victories, unmistakable miracles, and events that scream, "By this you will know that I am God."

At times, God is very specific about what He wants us to do. Sometimes He adjusts His approach because of people's failures. Divorce was never God's plan, but Jesus explained that since human hearts have become hardened, God has allowed people to divorce (see Matthew 19:3–9). Is part of God's ultimate plan people staying faithful to each other? Will that day come? As humanity learns the lessons of their choices, they will soon discover the best way to live as children of God's kingdom.

I think we will discover that God's plan—His will for our lives—may involve something entirely different from the color car you drive or the house you choose to live in or even which company you work for. God does very specifically reveal His will. We'll talk more about that later in the book.

Myth #3: If God wants to communicate with you, He'll give you a sign.

Khun Paot, a teenage girl, escaped the butchery of the Khmer Rouge in Cambodia after trekking through dangerous terrain with one hundred others who were seeking freedom. Filling the area between the company of travelers and safety were Communist soldiers, darkness, and a thorny jungle. The majority of the escapees had no shoes to protect their feet and no light to guide their way. Darkness hampered the tired group as they crossed a valley between two mountain ranges. When the blackness of night made them unable to take another step, hundreds of fireflies swarmed around the group. The fireflies produced enough light around the travelers that they could see each other, and most importantly, find their way. Later, in the refugee camp, Khun Paot was invited to a Christian gathering. Pointing to a picture of Jesus that hung on the wall, she exclaimed, "He's the One who showed us the way to Thailand and freedom by the light of the fireflies."

Stories like this prompt a wide assortment of responses, ranging from misty-eyed awe to the suspicious pause that wonders if the storyteller took an extra preaching class instead of Introduction to Ethics. Does this stuff really happen? Does God really enter into the time and space of our lives to communicate, guide, and reroute our steps?

Sometimes He *does* interrupt the routine with shiny displays of glory or a dramatic bombardment of His power. While most people never get to experience events such as this, they have happened and they do happen, and my guess is that they will happen again. But if you always expect it to happen *to you*, you might be disappointed. One enduring reality colors every glorious epiphany—God dramatically intervenes when you least expect it.

Often, a divine interruption is an attention-getting device. Anyone who wants God to write His message on their dining room wall should consider the nature and purpose of those little events: warning, rebuke, correction, instruction, intimidation, judgment. (Think about Daniel 5.) Be careful what you ask for. Do you really want to know what God sees in the future?

Throughout the Bible, we see moments in which God clearly gives people supernatural evidence of His plan. The New Testament alone contains many instances in which God makes clear what His will is:

- The disciples on the road to Emmaus
- Philip and the Ethiopian
- Saul on the road to Damascus
- Paul and Silas in prison

These were moments when God stepped in—not metaphorically, not figuratively, but unmistakably. The reason we need to check this myth is that sometimes we think that since God has done this before, He must do it the same way, always. When God does speak and intervene dramatically, it tends to be when we are about to make a grave error or when He has a unique request.

If God can best communicate His purpose by fire, then fire is fine with Him. But Elijah's experience is an important lesson that God doesn't always choose to communicate with people the same way. As a matter of course, He shakes things up a bit. On one mountain that Elijah climbed, God spoke through fire. So, Elijah waited on another mountain. But God's voice wasn't in the fire, the wind, or the earthquake. Instead, He chose to speak in what the Bible says was "a still, small voice" (see 1 Kings 19:9–14). The Hebrew word can be translated as "calm" or even "silent." Either way, the idea is that God spoke profoundly in a not-so-dramatic way.

Some signs can distract instead of communicating. When I went to Australia on a speaking assignment, I noticed a sign that read "Uniting Church Meets at Deception Bay." I thought that was interesting. Still more confusing was the sign I saw posted by a driveway at Taco Bell that read "Drive Thru Window." I hadn't considered driving through the window to get a quick, cheap meal, but it sounds like an option. I had often wondered why highway workers always look so dejected until I read signs littering the road that announced "Slow Men at Work." And I was amused by a sign that was attached to a fence in an industrial yard. The sign read "No Smoking Hazardous Chemicals."

The point is that signs can communicate messages that weren't intended. For people to operate under the assumption that God will give us a sign when we have to make an important decision or when we don't know what to do may be one of those faulty notions to which we cling.

Guidance from the gut

The saying "What does your gut tell you?" isn't just a saying. The ancients considered examining internal components of living beings an acceptable method for seeking a sign from the gods. In Ezekiel, we get a glimpse of pagan rituals for seeking wisdom: "The word of the LORD came to me: 'Son of man, mark out two roads for the sword of the king of Babylon to take, . . . For the king of Babylon will stop at the fork in the road, at the junction of the two roads, to seek an omen: He will cast lots with arrows, he will consult his idols, he will examine the liver' " (21:18–21).

OK, that's gross. But the pagan world made a science of determining the will of the gods. Shooting an arrow into the air to discover which way to go is a method called *rhabdomancy*. Idols to which people offer sacrifices for the purpose of gaining favor or seeking advice were called *teraphim*. But at that time, the method of choice for seeking heavenly wisdom was to examine the liver of sheep. Bruce Waltke discusses this phenomenon: "Pagans devised all sorts of special tasks to help them determine the mind of God. Each of those tasks included searching for some special sign given by the gods. The most popular was *hepatoscopy*, the study of the liver. Pagans believed that memory and intelligence resided in the liver, not the brain, and they created an entire course of study to read livers. The liver was the heaviest organ, and therefore if God was going to reveal His mind to man He would do so through the heaviest and supposedly most important organ."[3]

Many innocent sheep have been slaughtered in times of war or uncertainty for the purpose of discovering God's plan. Laugh all you want, but it was a common practice.

The ancient assumption that God will and must speak through a sign is a powerful underpinning to the thought process of believers and unbelievers alike. Daniel Schaeffer muses, "Signs are hard to figure sometimes. We think we know what they mean, but what happens when they don't turn out to mean what they thought? We are a sign-conscious people, constantly looking for them to determine what to do next."[4] Think about how many times you have wondered whether an event was a sign from God. The unexpected phone call. An unanticipated visitor. A check in the mailbox. An acceptance letter. A job offer. A random act of kindness. A clean bill of health.

Several questions surface when you stir up the conversation about miraculous communiqués from the finger of God. What determines whether a sign is a sign? How does a person distinguish between supernatural events and coincidences? Even if God were to give you a sign for guidance, how would you know what it means? Why doesn't God give you a sign every time you are confused? Are some moments in life more "sign-worthy" than others?

The bottom line is that signs may be impressive, but they aren't always what they seem to be. Schaeffer illustrates this truth:

> During the war, the logistics of supply in the Pacific Theatre were complicated by the fact that U.S. pilots had to fly long distances over open water. Cargo planes were often forced to crash-land, or simply crash, on remote islands, some inhabited by natives who had never seen an airplane up close, much less the stuff we Americans packed in one: food in cans, ready-made clothes, radios, medicine. After the war this phenomenon ended. But the hope did not. A kind of religion grew up called the "cargo cult." Believers worshipped the big metal birds, those that were rusting away in the jungle, and those that flew overhead—praying they would crash and bestow their magical cargoes on them again. They never did.[5]

While the Bible contains examples of God directing people with signs, are these the exception or the rule? Look at the purpose of the signs and wonders throughout the Bible and ask, "What is God's purpose in this event?" Paul explained, "Since in the wisdom of God the world through its wisdom *did not know him*, God was pleased through the foolishness of what was preached to save those who believe. Jews demand miraculous signs and Greeks look for wisdom, but we preach Christ crucified" (1 Corinthians 1:21–23, emphasis added). According to Paul, God is mostly interested in being known.

Some "believe" only when it makes sense; others "believe" because of a miracle. But there's no guarantee that knowledge or even a truckload of supernatural fireworks is going to cause people to respond to God. Consider this principle at work in the parable of the rich man and Lazarus. The rich man pleads with Abraham to send Lazarus to his family and personally warn them to avoid the predicament in which his selfish lifestyle has landed him. But Abraham reminds the rich man that his family has "Moses and the prophets" (God's revealed Word) to consider as a guide for life. Pressing the issue one step further, the rich man begs Abraham to send someone from the dead, for surely a representative from the hereafter would convince them to live right. But Abraham soberly reminds the rich man, " 'If they do not listen to Moses and the Prophets, they will not be convinced even if someone rises from the dead' " (Luke 16:31).

Clearly, the lesson is that the sign had already been given in the pages of God's Word. Not even a ghost from the afterlife will cause people to change. Steven Curtis Chapman wrote this truth in the song "Waiting for Lightning." He sings,

> The sign and the word
> Have already been given
> And now it's by faith
> That we must look, and we must listen.

And his song warns, "You're listening for thunder / While He quietly whispers your name."

Signs and wonders are dangerous places to put your trust for two reasons: First, because we may simply be looking for "signs" that justify what we want. And second, because Satan's agencies may be able to fabricate wonders to draw us away from God's revealed Word. Jesus warned His disciples, " 'False Christs and false prophets will appear and perform great signs and miracles to deceive even the elect—if that were possible' " (Matthew 24:24). And referring to the satanic agencies that will deceive the world in the final events of earth's history, John the revelator said that in his vision they "performed great and miraculous signs, even causing fire to come down from heaven to earth in full view of men. Because of the signs he was given power to do on behalf of the first beast, he deceived the inhabitants of the earth" (Revelation 13:13, 14).

Looking for a sign is exhausting. When do you look? Where and how long? What constitutes a supernatural message? Some say, "You will know when it happens." Frankly, that is the most unsatisfying answer I have ever heard. At best, we tend to be inconsistent with what we trust to be truth in our lives. In our day and age, it isn't surprising to change from being a hardcore skeptic one moment to being phenomenon-focused and sign-silly the next.

A friend of mine, who happens to be a self-proclaimed atheist, barely survived a horrible automobile accident. Everyone from the emergency responders to the insurance agents deemed the fact that he survived the accident evidence of divine intervention. In the hospital, my friend's first statement to me was "Do you think God is trying to get my attention?" He was somber and teachable, willing to be open to new ideas—until he was back on his feet. Then his testimony changed from God seeking to get his attention to the effectiveness of airbags. How fickle.

As we look at God's will for our lives, we need to recognize that He may choose to guide people to trust in Him through the miraculous, or He may not. Jesus soon tired of trying to "prove Himself" through the miraculous signs people persistently demanded:

- " 'Unless you people see miraculous signs and wonders,' Jesus told him, 'you will never believe' " (John 4:48).
- "Then some of the Pharisees and teachers of the law said to him, 'Teacher, we want to see a miraculous sign from you.'

  "He answered, 'A wicked and adulterous generation asks for a miraculous sign! But none will be given it except the sign of the prophet Jonah' " (Matthew 12:38, 39).
- "Then the Jews demanded of him, 'What miraculous sign can you show us to prove your authority to do all this?'

  "Jesus answered them, 'Destroy this temple, and I will raise it again in three days' " (John 2:18, 19).

Again, if we consider what we know from Scripture about "signs and wonders," it seems that signs can often distract people from what

God has already declared. To be fair, it is notable that signs often helped some people believe that Jesus was worth listening to. (See, for example, John 2:23, 24; 6:14; 10:40–42; Acts 2:22, 23.) However, one of the problems with seeking signs is the tendency to focus on the sign alone instead of what it is pointing to. One of my students returned from visiting a church that believes the spiritual gift of speaking in tongues is a sign of the indwelling Holy Spirit. Church members had asked him, "Have you received the Spirit?" The question puzzled him because it was clear that they considered "having the Spirit" and speaking in tongues to constitute a package deal. How troubling it is when people emphasize attaining a specific spiritual gift rather than the purpose of the gift.

It's clear in Scripture that God uses these miraculous moments of communication to serve His purpose. He chooses when He will communicate through signs and wonders. If you find yourself wondering if your flat tire is a sign from God about who you should marry, you might reconsider some of your assumptions about how God guides. Sometimes we get a flat tire because there was a nail in the road. With such strong warnings from Christ Himself about looking for signs, it behooves us to examine how reasonable it is to expect God to light up a bush every time we need some direction.

Remember . . .

- God determines when signs and wonders are necessary to our understanding and believing His will.
- While God has used signs to demonstrate His goodness and power, He has clearly communicated His will in tangible, less sensational ways for the purpose of fostering our faith in Him.
- When supernatural interruptions do occur, they are usually unmistakable and serve the purpose of getting someone's attention.
- Jesus downplays signs and wonders, especially if they take the place of obedience to His Word.

Some roads where I live have rumble strips that warn you when you're crossing into oncoming traffic or off the side of the road. But not all of the roads where I live have those bumps. Sometimes staying on the road means keeping your eyes open and your hands on the wheel.

Unfortunately, the business of seeing God's will is rarely ever perfectly clear. It is important to note that although we can't see the way perfectly, we can still see well enough.

Myth #4: God gave you a brain, and He expects you to make it the basis of all your decision-making.

If the modern world has gifted humanity with anything, it is an increased opinion of its own opinion. We call it reason and rational thinking, but boil it down to its most central element and you'll find "logical" or "scientific" guesses about what is good, right, real, and meaningful. As the Age of Reason dawned on humanity, people shifted their thinking from "God is the source and center of human experience" to "God is peripheral, and my perceptions are what is most real." The human mind, with its ability to reason, invented solutions to some of our problems and discovered answers for some of our questions. This became our focus during the period often referred to as "the Enlightenment."

While human thinking moved many away from the notion that there is a God, it gave others, who remained believers, a strong sense that if God has a plan for our lives, the way to discover it is through good decision-making and wisdom. They concluded that miraculous interpositions are simply not to be expected or believed.

These underpinnings of the modern age are still alive and well today. One study reports that nearly 60 percent of respondents "strongly agree/believe that 'when you make a major decision, God wants you to make the best possible decision based on logically evaluating all of the options.' Another 24 percent agree 'somewhat with this notion.' "[6]

Throughout the history of humankind, God has expected people to use the brain He has given them to discern right from wrong and what is best from what is not good at all. In the same way that providence and signs can be modes of God's guidance, so can our minds. But if you depend entirely upon one mode of communication alone, you narrow the options of communication in the same way the puppy did when it waited for squirrels to drop from the tree. When you determine that you will listen only one way, you are predetermining the way God can speak to you.

One way you can always count on God speaking to you is through His Word. One of the qualities Scripture credits the Bereans as having was their willingness to test the words of people against the Word of God: "Now the Bereans were of more noble character than the Thessalonians, for they received the message with great eagerness and examined the Scriptures every day to see if what Paul said was true" (Acts 17:11, 12).

The Bereans' "eagerness" was a teachable spirit that was hungry for truth and direction. This stood in contrast to the spiritual leaders in Christ's day who knew the Scriptures backward and forward but failed to connect their knowledge to the person of Christ who stood before them: " 'You diligently study the Scriptures because you think that by them you possess eternal life. These are the Scriptures that testify about me, yet you refuse to come to me to have life' " (John 5:39, 40). How could they not see? I think the wise man captured it well when he said, "There is a way that seems right to a man, / but in the end it leads to death" (Proverbs 14:12). Reason plays a role in understanding the will of God. But there are times when all the clear thinking in the world doesn't make God's will any easier to understand and do:

- Building an ark when no one has ever seen rain, a flood, or even anything remotely resembling a natural disaster
- Assembling an army based upon the drinking style of the soldiers
- As a teenage boy, taking on a giant in battle
- Sacrificing on an altar the son whom God sent to be the father of a whole nation
- Dipping seven times in the river to remove the disease of leprosy
- As a virgin, conceiving a child by the Holy Spirit

At some point, we simply have to throw the book of human wisdom out because the wisdom of God confounds the wisdom of man. God can lead those who are teachable in the same way He led Noah, Abraham, Moses, David, and Mary. In all their stories, it was never a case of brains versus God's mysterious leading but a cooperation between the two. Consider David for a moment. When we read in 1 Samuel 17:24 that the Israelites ran from Goliath's challenge "in great fear," it becomes clear that they all had done the math and had come to the same conclusion: Fighting Goliath wasn't wise—a clear and fast "no brainer." But sometimes everyone is wrong. What appears to be human wisdom can be a very dubious form of knowledge.

In a classroom experiment, teachers wrote several words on the blackboard. Then they pointed to a word and asked if it was spelled correctly, and the class voted thumbs up for Yes and thumbs down for No. However, before the class met, the teachers had prompted all the students but one to vote No on a word that was spelled correctly in the last list. In most of the classrooms where this experiment was conducted, the solitary students voted with the majority in spite of their initial sensibilities.

David wouldn't be swayed in the same way. He wasn't listening only to the data displayed at the battlefield. He was also hearing the Voice to which he accorded authority. David measured the words of Saul the king, Goliath the giant, and all the men of Israel by what he knew to be true about God.

However, taking on Goliath wasn't a *mindless* leap of faith when you consider the encounters David had experienced with lions and bears. It must have looked mindless to some, but imagine how heaven roared with pride as David "ran quickly to the battle line to meet him." When he chased down Goliath, he wasn't on some spiritually psychotic rampage. Rather, he was listening to a different voice—a voice that is not easily heard by conventional wisdom.

In the life of David and of many others throughout history, God sometimes makes a mess of human wisdom and causes us all to leave a little room for the unimaginable to happen. While there are moments when God has called people to trust His Word more than conventional wisdom, these moments rarely involve suspending the sense of discernment. The two never seem to be mutually exclusive. Maybe the assumption that God wants us to use our brain and make good choices isn't faulty at all. But knowing what we know about humanity, can we be totally confident in human wisdom alone?

All of this reminds me of a true, yet tragic, World War II story. The *Lady Be Good* was a famous bomber flown by a team of well-seasoned, combat-savvy airmen. After their final successful mission, they made their way home during the night. The instruments and other navigational aids were available to help the crew reach their destination. But they had flown this route so many times before that they barely consulted them.

As the bomber proceeded through the night, the crew was unaware that a strong tailwind was propelling them more rapidly than usual. They were shocked when the instruments signaled it was time to land. Refusing to rely on the accuracy of the gauges, they continued through the night, confident that they still had many miles to go. They became concerned when they couldn't see the lights and the markers they usually used as a guide on their journey. By the time they realized that they had significantly overshot their destination, their fuel supply was so depleted that they couldn't make it back to the airfield. The *Lady Be Good* was found several days later in the desert, well beyond their destination. The entire crew perished because they rested entirely on their own wisdom.

It is possible to be sure of something that seems so right but proves to be so wrong. What happened in the air back in the early 1940s is happening in principle when we base our decisions solely on brainpower. Brains can be wrong.

Have you considered the many stories and scenarios that occurred in Scripture that simply were not logical, reasonable, or rational according to human wisdom? Note the insight that comes from God to a wise guy,

> "Blessed is the man who listens to me,
> watching daily at my doors,
> waiting at my doorway" (Proverbs 8:34).

Listening, watching, waiting at the very doorway of God. This might be the most salient wisdom available on being guided by God.

What do you believe about the way God will convey His will to you? What are your expectations? What are the methods you think He will use? Which do you tend to rely on the most? Understanding our assumptions about God's will and the way He guides us is an essential step to discovering God's will and living it.

While God's will may seem like a mystery to us or a puzzle full of missing pieces, God doesn't play hide-and-seek with His children. He does have a dream for each person, and He claims to know the future, but He also meets people in their mistakes as well as in their moments of greatness, and He leads them into a good life.

Can God's perfect plan really be about making the right decision all the time? Does one mistake disqualify me from plan A? Is it really His standard operating procedure to reveal Himself through signs and wonders? I can think of many times I was so sure I was right, but my human wisdom failed me. So, before we go much further, it's time that we check our assumptions at the door.

1. J. I. Packer, *God's Plans for You* (Wheaton, Ill.: Crossway Books, 2001), 91.

2. Jerry Sittser, *Discovering God's Will* (Grand Rapids, Mich.: Zondervan, 2000), 17.

3. Bruce Waltke, *Knowing the Will of God for the Decisions in Life* (Eugene, Ore.: Harvest House Publishers, 1998), 31.

4. Daniel Schaeffer, *The Bush Won't Burn and I'm All Out of Matches: How to Find God's Will When You Have Looked Everywhere* (Grand Rapids, Mich.: Discovery House Publishers, 1995), 8.

5. Ibid., 7, 8.

6. Robert Jeffress, *Hearing the Master's Voice: The Comfort and Confidence of Knowing God's Will* (Colorado Springs, Colo.: WaterBrook Press, 2001), 211.

Questions for Reflection

1. What are some myths or urban legends that you assumed were true?

2. Of the myths about God's will discussed in this chapter, which do you think is most pervasive?

3. In what way has God's will seemed like a puzzle to you?

4. Think of a time in your life when you perceived that one decision could establish you in or break you away from God's will.

5. To what degree do you think God expects people to use their brains to find His will for their life? When have you faced a dilemma in which the "logical choice" turned out not to be the best choice?

6. Have you ever experienced what you thought was a sign from God? How did you respond?

Guiding Principles

The human search for God's will can be compared to the drama of trying to find the most efficient line at the grocery store. There I am, scanning the groceries of those checking out, to see which line is likely to move the fastest. I conclude that the carts in checkout lane four have fewer items than those in any other lane, so I wheel my cart of about eighteen items over there. Then it happens. "Price check on four." The call sounds again and again, until finally a bagger emerges from an aisle and receives instructions to check the price on a can of sliced olives. The choice of checkout lane four has turned out to be a bad one.

I quickly scan the options, back my cart out of line, and proceed to lane six. But another shopper with a cart pregnant with groceries slides into that lane just before me. I look back to see my previous position in lane four swallowed up by eager shoppers who avoid my glance but wear what seem to be smirks of pleasure as my misfortune becomes their pleasant surprise.

After assessing the available lanes, I choose one with promise. At this point, the little old lady at the front of the line erupts, "I have a coupon for that." Then she searches through a stack of coupons about the size of a deck of cards. The people in front of me groan, but hope springs from an angel wearing a store smock who grabs my cart and says, "I'll take you on lane seven." And this miracle from heaven guides my cart to lane seven, where there are no other customers except for the frantic throng lining up behind me.

I place my items on the counter and watch as she scans each one quickly. I glance at the smirkers in lane four to see where I am in the race—I mean process—and it is dead even. Then, with only six items left to scan, the cash register starts to gurgle and sputter, and it emits tape with a red line on it. "Oh, I'm out of tape," the cashier exclaims, and she looks at me as though in terrible pain. But her sympathy is for herself, not for me. She whines, "This always happens to me," and I want to explode. "*You?* Do you have any idea what *I've* been through? I've been price-checked, closed off, merged out, and cold-stalled by the president of the coupon collectors' club. And just when I think I'm getting a break, you run out of tape!" And the smirkers saunter by without looking at me.

This story reminds me of the approach we often take in our search for God's will. We know there is a will and there must be a way, but when the complexities of life short-circuit every way we choose, we become frustrated. Furthermore, there don't seem to be guiding principles that work consistently. We pray—but receive no direct response. We take a leap of faith—and land in need of assistance. We obey God's Word—and are misunderstood. We ask for advice—and are unsatisfied with the guidance. We look for signs—and become frustrated by the obvious lack of supernatural communication. We try to use our brains—but there are too many things about the future that we don't know. We make all the right choices—and still the bottom drops out of our life.

I've read the books that prescribe a recipe for success in looking to God to guide the way. They promise, "Seven easy steps to knowing what to do with your life." "Four checkpoints to determining God's will." I'm not always sure it is good to enumerate "the way," but I will share a few proverbs that may help in our search. I'm certain there are more, but these will provide a good start.

Proverb #1: Don't let what you don't know confuse you about what you do know.

One particular story from the ministry of Christ keenly illustrates this proverb. The entire story is contained in John 9; I will summarize the encounter: Jesus and the disciples happen upon a man who has been blind from birth. The disciples want to know why. Was it he or his parents who sinned? Jesus seizes the moment for a lesson in God's glory. He spits, makes mud, plasters it on the eyes of the man, and tells him to wash it off. The man does, and he receives his sight. Everyone wonders what happened, and the man tells them what Jesus had him do. The Pharisees investigate. They hastily conclude that since this was done on the Sabbath, it was not of God. The accusations create confusion and more inquiry. The parents are questioned. Frightened by the pressure, they defer and say, "Ask him." The Pharisees roar at the man, "What did He do to you? How did He open your eyes?"

We pick up the central point of the story—the answer of the man who was born blind: " 'Whether he is a sinner or not, I don't know. One thing I do know. I was blind but now I see' " (verse 25). Clearly, this man has the ability to keep in mind what he knows and to avoid confusing it with what he doesn't know. The Pharisees display the complete opposite attributes; they're short-circuited by what they don't know. The Bible says, "They hurled insults at him and said, 'You are this fellow's disciple! We are disciples of Moses! We know that God spoke to Moses, but as for this fellow, we don't even know where he comes from' " (verses 28, 29). They conclude that Jesus and His works are of the devil because He is a no-name teacher operating on a different program than they are.

The man born blind catches their mistake and calls them on their faulty thinking: " 'Now that is remarkable! You don't know where he comes from, yet he opened my eyes. We know that God does not listen to sinners. He listens to the godly man who does his will. Nobody has ever heard of opening the eyes of a man born blind. If this man were not from God, he could do nothing' " (verses 30–33).

To this, the Pharisees replied, " 'You were steeped in sin at birth; how dare you lecture us!' " (verse 34).

Well, there you have it. Before we sneer and scorn the Pharisees for being such nincompoops, we must ask whether we might possibly use the same thought process as they. Whether in the middle of a disaster or at the crossroads of a big decision, when we are faced with what we don't know, we're wise to remind ourselves of what we do know.

When I was a teenager, I suffered a painful season when I lost one of my best friends to cystic fibrosis. I was a new Christian at the time and couldn't understand why this would happen to such a kind and generous person. Unlike the man whose son was possessed, I couldn't reconcile my belief and my unbelief. My experience with God could be likened to the Dr. Jekyll and Mr. Hyde phenomenon. Then one of my teachers asked us to make a list of all the things we believed with certainty and all the things we really wondered about. And she asked a question that struck my senses like a lightning bolt: "What happens to your questions when you look at them in light of the things you are certain about?"

I remember thinking seriously about her query, and while my questions didn't dissolve away, I didn't see them as unbearable, nor did they undermine everything I believed. The perspective she suggested was liberating. I didn't ever clearly answer my question about why God let Diana die so young, but I was reminded that the same God who let my friend pass away brought my family and me out of darkness into the Christian life. The big question is, Can I live with that? (More about this in chapter 6.) The truth is, what we don't know doesn't have to erase what we do know. In fact, it's possible to examine the unknown from the known.

This proverb is much easier to say than it is to do, but try using it by writing down two columns on a piece of paper. In one column, write what you know, and in the other, what you don't know. Here are my lists:

What I Know	What I Don't Know
I believe there is a God who created the world, who loves humanity, and who gave His life to redeem them. I believe the Bible is His Word to people. I know God is going to come again. I know He has been good to me. I know He has answered some of my prayers.	I don't know why some innocent people suffer more than other people do. I don't know why some of God's followers are so unlike the God they describe. I don't understand why some prayers seem to be answered and some don't.

The Bible contains many examples of people who refused to allow the unknown to undermine the known. Peter, a skilled and knowledgeable fisherman, didn't know why Jesus asked him to throw out his nets again. Measuring what he knew about Jesus against what he was clearly uncertain of (fishing during midday), he stated, " 'Master, we've worked hard all night and haven't caught anything. But because you say so, I will let down the nets' " (Luke 5:5). There is no great moral dilemma here, only a man considering the questionable through the lens of his confidence in Christ.

On another occasion, Jesus delivered a hard message about eating His flesh and drinking His blood. His words caused a major mutiny in which "many of his disciples turned back and no longer followed him" (John 6:66). So, Jesus peered into the eyes of the Twelve and asked them if they were going to leave as well. This was a watershed moment for the disciples, because while it wasn't exactly clear where Jesus was taking His movement, it seemed to be going downhill quickly. Notice the response of the disciples: " 'Lord, to whom shall we go? You have the words of eternal life. We believe and know that you are the Holy One of God' " (verses 68, 69). My paraphrase would go like this: "We don't understand half the things You say, and it seems clear to us that You are steering this ship to sure destruction, but we have seen too much: too much grace. Too much truth. Too many miracles. Too many things make sense now that You are here, and that means what doesn't add up doesn't matter much to us anymore. So, since we believe You are God, we're in with You for the long haul."

In light of scenarios like this one, I'm uncomfortable with the phrase "blind faith." I'm uncomfortable with it only because when people respond as the disciples did, it's not because of blindness but rather because of another form of vision. Instead of operating on eyesight, they launch out because of insight. Based upon what they know, they negotiate through what they don't know about the world around them.

Think of the three Hebrew boys who fronted up to the king of Babylon. They knew God *could* miraculously spare their lives, but they didn't know that He *would*. Still, they acted on what they knew to be good, right, and true. They said that whether or not God spared them, they wouldn't worship the image. " 'If we are thrown into the blazing furnace, the God we serve is able to save us from it, and he will rescue us from your hand, O king. But even if he does not, we want you to know, O king, that we will not serve your gods or worship the image of gold you have set up' " (Daniel 3:17, 18).

The biblical stories like this one often seem so familiar, so natural to us. But living according to this proverb in our relationships, our beliefs, and our decisions about where to go and what to do is painfully challenging.

Proverb #2: Don't let what you can't see now obscure what has been revealed to you.

The San Joaquin Valley in Central California hosts seasons of extremely dense fog. Normally, driving home from school was a fifteen-minute, relatively mindless exercise for me. But when the fog was extreme, the drive home could be a serious drama.

One day the fog was so dense that I had to open my car door and look down at the dotted yellow line marking the center of the road to navigate my way. I was moving at about five miles an hour when brake lights abruptly lit up in front of me. I waited for a moment, but whoever was driving that car wasn't ready to move another meter in the fog. So I got out of my car and approached the next one, inquiring, "Are you all right?"

The window rolled down, and a frightened little old lady exclaimed, "I can't see. I know I'm old, but I'm not blind!"

I reassured her, affirming that driving was nearly impossible in these conditions.

"Is this Oakdale Road?" she continued. "I was on Oakdale Road, but I don't recognize anything. I don't know how far I've gone or how much farther I need to go to find the cross street. Can you see in this fog? Can I follow you somewhere?"

Her street was close to mine, so I guided her home. I knew we were on Oakdale Road because I had turned where I saw the sign and I hadn't left the road. But I couldn't see anything around me that affirmed that this was in fact the road I was supposed to be on. As I reflect on that event, I'm struck with how often I fail to act on this guiding principle. Often my circumstances and the absence of clarity completely erase everything I've seen before.

On another road, in what seemed to be a fog of biblical proportions, two nearly anonymous disciples tried to make their way through disappointment and confusion but found the way murky at best. Luke recorded the story in chapter 24 of his Gospel.

The travelers on the road to Emmaus were talking with each other about everything that had happened on the weekend of Jesus' crucifixion. As they talked about these things, Jesus Himself came up and walked along with them, but they were kept from recognizing Him. Then Jesus "asked them, 'What are you discussing together as you walk along?'

"They stood still, their faces downcast. One of them, named Cleopas, asked him, 'Are you only a visitor to Jerusalem and do not know the things that have happened there in these days?' " (verses 17, 18).

Several aspects of this exchange intrigue me. First, the disciples were talking over the events of the last seventy-two hours, and talking it over wasn't making things any clearer. With all the facts firmly in place, the whole episode was still as clear as mud to the travelers.

Second, the disciples questioned the mysterious hiker as if an outsider could possibly have as clear a view as devoted followers of Jesus. They asked, "Are you only a visitor to Jerusalem and do not know the things that have happened there in these days?" I can almost hear them thinking, "We walked with Him for years, and we don't get it. How could a tourist make sense of this?" Furthermore, it is so like human nature to be blind but still think you can see just fine. The more intense the conversation became and the more details they recited, the denser the fog seemed to them.

It gets better. Listen to their assessment of the whole ordeal about Jesus of Nazareth:

> "He was a prophet, powerful in word and deed before God and all the people. The chief priests and our rulers handed him over to be sentenced to death, and they crucified him; but we had hoped that he was the one who was going to redeem Israel. And what is more, it is the third day since all this took place. In addition, some of our women amazed us. They went to the tomb early this morning but didn't find his body. They came and told us that they had seen a vision of angels, who said he was alive. Then some of our companions went to the tomb and found it just as the women had said, but him they did not see" (verses 19–24).

So, what's the problem? He "was a prophet"—a prophet like Moses. He was "powerful in word and deed"—what better way to convey a "teacher with authority"—unlike the Pharisees and priests. He was arrested and crucified—right again. The disciples even articulated the rumors that confirmed the very words Jesus had spoken only a few days earlier. They recounted all the marvelous things Jesus said and did to the letter. They parroted the words Jesus had told them when He prophesied that He would be " 'handed over to the chief priests and rulers and would be sentenced to death but raised three days later.' "

This story demonstrates a sad truth about people: We can be blind and still think we see clearly. We can be confused and think the lapse in logic is somewhere other than in our thinking. We can be exposed to unmistakable evidence and make the mistake of seeing it wrong. Don't you just want to shout, "Hello! The truth is right in front of you. What are you—blind?"

Listen carefully to the disciples when they report, " 'We had hoped that he was the one who would redeem Israel.' " Evidently, this is where things went awry. Even in light of the centuries of ceremonial sacrifices, the fact that this redemption was purchased on a Roman cross is inconceivable to the disciples. Their assumption about redemption—what it is and how it would come about—disabled their entire framework for viewing the truth that was standing right in front of them. So, Jesus walks them through the whole story, starting at the beginning: "He said to them, 'How foolish you are, and how slow of heart to believe all that the prophets have spoken! Did not the Christ have to suffer these things and then enter his glory?' And beginning with Moses and all the Prophets, he explained to them what was said in all the Scriptures concerning himself" (verses 25–27).

The problem was not the sureness of these disciples' eyes, but the stubbornness of their hearts to embrace the way God had clearly guided them in the past. Don't let what you can't see now obscure what has been revealed to you. When the way ahead is unclear, back up and survey the revelation of God in history, in your life, and in His Word. Sometimes, the only way to negotiate the future is to remember the evidence that litters the trail behind you.

Notice that the disciples credit aspects of God's revelation for finally opening their eyes: First, they recognized Jesus after "he took bread, gave thanks, broke it and began to give it to them" (verse 30). This familiar scene that was lodged so deeply in their hearts emerged only when they witnessed it again.

And second, God's Word brought about a deep response in their hearts. They asked each other, " 'Were not our hearts burning within us while he talked with us on the road and opened the Scriptures to us?' " (verse 32). The information and wisdom from Scripture became central to their worldview again. Sometimes in our most confusing moments, our cognitive sensibilities take a vacation.

The case of heartburn these two disciples experienced launched them back down the road—the opposite direction they had just traveled.

When my circumstances are like a dense fog, retracing my steps and re-minding myself of the guidance along the way guides me in the right direction. Sometimes, that right direction is an about-face.

I don't think I've ever heard God speak audibly as some profess. But God has revealed Himself to me in ways that are real—so much more real than a shiver down my spine. Has God not revealed Himself to you in prayers that He answered, in providential moments—even in mira-cles? How about the way God has provided, sheltered, and guided you throughout your life up to this point, to your reading this book? Can you look back and not see how He has revealed Himself to you?

For every mean person in the church, there are a dozen sweet, grace-oriented, generous souls who smother you with affirmation. For every time you had to go without, there are countless times when God came through with the goods. As you are reading this book right now, it may be that you have prayed for blessing, protection, and perhaps traveling mercies. And while you may have experienced times when those prayers were seemingly unanswered, you probably wouldn't be reading this book today if there weren't a whole host of quiet, nondramatic moments in which God *has* answered.

Some say that God's will is often clearer in the rearview mirror than it is on the road ahead. If this is true, then what might be missing are reflective moments in which we consider the ways God has led us in the past. It may be that we have trouble remembering the times when God has been good to us because we rarely discipline ourselves to reflect upon and cement those moments in our memories.

Proverb #3: Don't let your aspirations for the future distract you from what you can do today.

Why do we feel like we have to know the future in order to do what we know is necessary right now? Think of the way Noah faced up to the daunting task of building an ark, and Moses leading a nation of three million people out of bondage, and David being anointed to replace the first king of Israel. We see their storied lives and their heroic victories, but we see them in hindsight. What we don't always notice is that Noah had to go to work on Monday morning with the neighbors laughing every time he broke a fingernail or cut a board just a hair too short. What makes Noah's legacy so profound is not the ark, the Flood, the animals, and the rainbow, but the fact that he went to work every day and did the little things. Noah was what I call a "day-Today" kind of believer.

What made Moses popular was the Red Sea. What made him a great leader was his willingness to stay in the wilderness for forty years tending sheep. Before Moses topped the list of MVPs, he was fulfilling his list of things to do today on a grassy hill somewhere.

David demonstrated his willingness to be about the business of the kingdom "today." When God needed him to play a song, he played a song. When God needed him to take out a giant, David was prepared to be God's man today. People who desperately clamor for the dream often miss the little moments that would make them great because they are so focused on greatness.

Consider what Abraham really had to go on. God basically told him, "Walk in that general direction over there and I will make a great nation out of you, more numerous than the stars in the sky"—though it may be that more happened between the divine calling and the heroic ending than we realize. However, we need to live the will of God today. What He has dreamed for each of us for tomorrow won't become a reality if we don't faithfully respond to what He wants for us today. Sometimes the connection between the menial stuff of today and the grand design of tomorrow are inconceivable—unless you learn to connect the dots.

When my good friend Dr. Jack and I venture out on a short-term mission trip, Dr. Jack has the team pack pills. We count the pills. We bag the pills. We label the pills. We dispense the pills. But do we connect the pills to something greater than the seemingly mindless task of preparing a pharmacy? Once I overheard some students dealing humorously with this dilemma. Holding one pill up reverently in the light, one of the students said, "I adjure thee, oh demon of bilharzia, to flee from the body of the one who swallows this pill!" Another incanted, "May the destructive power of infection be rendered impotent by thee, oh mighty Zithromax!" And the others chimed in with similar chants banishing the evil of malaria and of other known and unknown tropical diseases.

At first, I thought it was a bit irreverent, and it might have been, but what I loved in their little display was the connection they made between the significance of the little things we do today to the impact it has on a real person in pain. Obviously, the work of healing involves more than a pill. There is pain, seeking help, the gentle touch of a doctor, probing questions, insightful analysis, prayer, weighing of options, prescriptions, hope, instructions, ingestion, follow-through, restoration, strength, and ultimately, healing. But the pill is part of it—part of the heroic ability to embrace God's will for today and connect it to tomorrow.

I was interviewing kindergarten graduates about their aspirations. "What does the future hold for you?" I inquired of one lad.

"I'm going to be a big, strong fireman," he said with grim determination.

"How does one become a big, strong fireman?" I asked.

The sandy-haired boy replied with a knowing grin, "You have to eat your vegetables and get big and strong, and then you can pour all the water from the ocean on the world when Jesus sets it on fire."

I could barely refrain from laughing at his answer. What amused me most was the way he captured the moment when a firefighter would most be needed. Then, choosing not to chastise him for going head to head with Jesus at the time of the destruction of the wicked, I asked, "What do you think you should do today to be ready for such a big responsibility?"

He thought for a moment and answered confidently, "Eat my vegetables."

Is it possible that whatever great things the future holds for us, there will always be something to do today that is God's will?

When people ask me, "Why doesn't God just show where I am supposed to go and what I am supposed to do?" I reflect on those who have gone before and their perspective. I asked a successful executive in my community if he ever dreamed that he would be doing what he is doing now. He replied, "I had dreams, but they didn't look like this."

If someone had told you fifteen years ago what you would be doing today, would you have believed it? I asked a fellow pastor what he would have thought if God had told him when he was in college that he would be pastor of a large church and loving what he was doing. He replied, "I would have thought either God was joking or someone had slipped me a hallucinogen." God doesn't disclose the specifics about the future because most of the time we wouldn't believe Him.

Imagine asking Saul, the one who became Paul, if he dreamed as a young person he would become the most articulate voice for a radical movement. What if you had slipped in the news that one day millions of people would surrender their life to God because of the letters he would write? What about Mother Teresa? What do you think she would have said if you had told her when she was twenty that one day her name would become synonymous with being kind to someone in need? Or Martin Luther King Jr.? Take the time machine back, catch him as a nineteen-year-old graduate of high school, and encourage him to be diligent because the whole country would one day recognize his leadership as a pivotal point of the civil rights movement and that the country would create a holiday to memorialize his work. How do you think these great people would respond?

The big things of tomorrow rarely "just happen." They're made by the moment-by-moment, day-to-day decisions we make today. Paul punches the point home when he says, "Be very careful, then, how you live—not as unwise but as wise, *making the most of every opportunity*, because the days are evil" (Ephesians 5:15, 16, emphasis added). The author of Hebrews exhorts believers to "encourage one another daily, *as long as it is called Today*" (Hebrews 3:13, emphasis added). Furthermore, Jesus offers this maxim about the day-Today approach to life, saying, " 'Do not worry about tomorrow, for tomorrow will worry about itself. Each day has enough trouble of its own' " (Matthew 6:34). I don't think Jesus was trying to be negative when He used the word *trouble*. I believe He was referring to the way people get so far ahead of themselves with worry that they never live in the present.

Don't let your aspirations for the future distract you from doing what you can do today. What is so powerful about this principle is that it requires immediate action. The day-Today approach demands that we do what we can and should do now. Often, the only time we seek God's guidance is when we are stuck in neutral. Sometimes life smacks us upside the head so hard that we're paralyzed by the events that occur, and fear or uncertainty keeps us from moving forward and doing what needs to be done now. God will guide us in those moments, but the guidance may come only when we take action. Jane Kise puts it rather well: "Picture yourself in the driver's seat of a car. No matter how hard you crank the wheels, you can't change the direction it's pointed unless you first put it in gear, though, even if it is barely moving, even if the only propulsion comes from a few strong bodies pushing the vehicle from behind, turning the steering wheel will turn a moving car."[1]

The dilemma that a friend of mine faced while we were working at summer camp illustrates the proactive value of doing today what you know you should do. David had taken both the MCAT and the LSAT tests and scored high enough on both to be accepted into both programs, and he was struggling with the decision about which direction to go. He admitted, "I almost didn't come to work at camp this summer because I didn't know what to do, but I have all summer to make a choice, so I thought I would do what I have done for the last four years." That summer, as David worked as a counselor, he was inundated with cabinfuls of kids who had health issues. By the end of the summer, he knew he wanted to become a pediatrician.

Think of Moses marching his way to Pharaoh's palace. Previously, he'd whined to God about not knowing what to say. Did he have all the words rehearsed as he made his way to the city? Was the script placed firmly in his mind? God needed a man who would go today. And when Moses spoke, it was clear that God had guided him to the place he was supposed to be.

Often, the guidance we so earnestly seek comes only when we move forward with what we think is good, right, and true for today. When I headed out for my first serious year of college, I was making a journey of faith from the West Coast to the state of Tennessee. It was a journey of faith because I had only about $275 for gas and expenses, and my pickup truck had well over a hundred thousand miles under the hood. My entrance fee was covered by a scholarship I'd received for a year of service abroad, so I knew I could get started once I got there, but I had no assurance that I would make it there. However, I believed if I moved forward, God would move in to guide and bless.

I did reach the college, but then I faced other financial problems—and God didn't move as quickly as I wished. I needed a job that would cover my tuition, and the passing of the first week of school found me still without one. I continued to interview for jobs, but it seemed that God had led me across the country to leave me stranded.

I had actually packed my bags and was ready to return home when someone suggested I check with the financial aid office. I checked. My hopes were soaring, because everyone was so nice and positive. But the bottom line was that they could do very little. Then, surrounded by my bags, I scoured the classified ads one last time. I prayed, "God, I will go on any interview, do anything—just help me get a job that will pay for college." And I added a "now" at the end of my prayer to avoid any confusion.

I saw one job opportunity that intrigued me. The ad was for someone to care for horses at an estate. I had worked at summer camp and could do the basics, so I called and got an interview.

As I drove up the long driveway with pristine white fencing on both sides, I knew God had come through for me. I praised Him audibly when I saw at the top of the hill a giant white Southern mansion. My truck barely made it up the hill, and I parked carefully between a red Porsche and a black limousine, leaving enough room so they wouldn't scratch my truck.

I waited for my interview in a gorgeous marble entryway with an elegant cherry-wood staircase that circled up to the next floor. I felt as though a pillar of fire had guided me directly to this place—until the owner of the house walked into the entryway congratulating a fellow classmate of mine warmly and saying, "I look forward to seeing you first thing Monday morning."

I was crushed. The owner (Mr. B) looked at me and said, "I'm sorry. I'm going to go with Alan for this job." I made my way to the door feeling as though God was playing an awful game with my life. But experience had taught me to move forward and let God guide, so I swallowed my pride and pressed further. "Do you have anything else? I need a job to pay for school." He looked thoughtfully at me and replied, "I do need someone to live here and take care of the house, the guests, and the meals—someone who would be willing to train with me every day so I can stay in shape. Do you think you might be interested in something like that?" I nodded and tried not to say too much for fear I might mess it up.

Mr. B talked with me about how he liked to fill this position by word of mouth because he had to find someone he could trust to live on the estate. I worked hard and loved that job more and more each day. I loved working for Mr. B because he was honest, straightforward, and very much aware of the people around him. But even though he was paying me more than any other job I could have found, I struggled to pay my school bill. I knew that if I was going to be a pastor, I couldn't afford massive student loans. So I informed Mr. B that I would be leaving at the break because I just couldn't afford to continue.

One evening, Mr. B called me into the great room and said, "Troy, I have noticed that something has been bothering you lately, so I asked around. I want you to do well in school, and I need you here. You're doing well, so I'm docking your pay."

I was taken aback by the last line. It seemed out of place. But before I could even ask for a clarification, he handed me a statement from the college showing that my tuition for the year had been paid in full. Then he said, "I want you to work hard for me here, and I want you to study hard and achieve the things that you want to achieve without worrying about the money."

I will never forget the wisdom that I gained from working at the estate. One of the more poignant lessons was that there will always be voices that freeze you up with fear and keep your feet from moving forward. But there will also always be something you can do today that will eventually contribute to your understanding about what to do in the future. So, if you will move forward today in spite of the urge to stay in neutral, God will guide your steps and honor your faith.

Proverb #4: Don't let the cost of doing God's will preoccupy your mind to the point that you forget its value.

I visited a class of business majors to share a few insights on leadership and making successful decisions. I'm not exactly sure why I was chosen, other than because the professor of the class was a friend of mine and I think he had returned from vacation ill prepared to teach, so he commissioned me into service.

To start the class, I held up an envelope and said, "I have several things I can share with you today, but what I think will be most valuable to you is the advice I have written and placed in this envelope. I'll sell the wisdom that waits here to whoever is willing to pay twenty bucks for it."

I looked around the class and saw that many were smirking, waiting and watching to see who would do such a ridiculous thing: pay someone they didn't know for advice that they couldn't see ahead of time—and do it in front of their peers. A young man in the middle of the class cut the tension by pulling out his wallet, fishing out a twenty-dollar bill, and handing it to me with the words, "I'll take it." There were cheers and jokes and jibes all around the room. While this young man was embarrassed, he was determined to obtain the wisdom that resided in the envelope.

Seizing the teachable moment, I said, "OK, great! We have a sucker— I mean an adventurous entrepreneur. Before I hand you the envelope, tell me why you're willing to cough up twenty bucks for a piece of advice you have never read before from someone you have never met before."

The class waited for his reply. He looked around the room, pointed to a stack of books on the desk, and said, "I bought and read those textbooks, which cost at least sixty bucks a piece, and I don't think there is anything terribly profound in them; they all say pretty much the same thing. I figured that after the hundreds of dollars I've spent on textbooks, trying something new was worth the risk. And I won't have to spend three weeks reading what's in that envelope to find out whether or not it was worth it."

I gave him the envelope, he gave me the twenty bucks, and I proceeded to go on with the class in a traditional manner. But the class roared at the young man. "Open it! We want to know what it says."

He opened the envelope and took out a small card that had two twenty-dollar bills taped to the back. He noticed that first, and he triumphantly showed everyone in the class his 100 percent profit. Then he read the card silently to himself and said, "Whoa, that's good." At that, the class erupted with curiosity and threatened to beat the advice out of him—which I don't think is good business practice. So, the young man read the words penned on the card: "If you want to be successful in life, shift your thinking from what you might lose to what you might gain."

One truth that always emerges from that exercise is that all of us should know what we value. I'm talking the worth, not the price tag. In our world, everything seems to have a price tag, but successful people see the value. A four-wheel-drive vehicle may cost forty thousand dollars, but what is it worth? For someone who commutes every day or who has to park in small spaces, the vehicle may not be worth the cost. My wife has been in thirteen accidents (none of which were her fault). She feels safer and more secure sitting up high, where she can see better and react quicker to the road ahead. How much is that worth? What about a college education? It's pretty expensive. Is a degree worth a hundred thousand dollars?

In 1775, Patrick Henry made the timeless declaration of what the cause of freedom was worth to him. He said, "Give me liberty, or give me death." The price of freedom was expensive, but the value of freedom was worth it. Everything depends on what people believe the object they are pursuing to be worth. We need to look at value instead of being guided by price. If we don't, we might know the price of everything and the value of nothing.

Jesus used two parables to fasten the truth of this principle in the minds of His followers: " 'The kingdom of heaven is like treasure hidden in a field. When a man found it, he hid it again, and then in his joy went and sold all he had and bought that field. Again the kingdom of heaven is like a merchant looking for fine pearls. When he found one of great value, he went away and sold everything he had and bought it' " (Matthew 13:44–46).

The first parable says that in the routine of the day, a man accidentally stumbled on something incredibly valuable. Evidently, he'd been hired to plow a field. But when he discovered treasure, he sold everything in order to get enough money to purchase the field and obtain the treasure. What Christ offered those who would receive Him and follow Him was worth the cost they would have to pay. His challenge: Think not about how much it costs but about how much it's worth to you.

The only contrast in the parable of the pearl of great price is that instead of stumbling on the precious treasure, the individual involved had been deliberately searching for it. The merchant knew what he was looking for, and when he discovered it, he traded in everything to acquire it. Maybe Jesus told the two parables to include both the seekers and the stumblers in the journey of life.

What is your hidden treasure? What is your pearl of great price? What matters most to you? What do you treasure more than anything else? What are you willing to do or give to gain your greatest desire? What treasures do you now possess that will become trinkets "compared to the surpassing greatness of following Christ"? Those were the words Paul used to describe what a saving relationship with Jesus was worth to him. Consider how clear his sense of value is:

"Whatever was to my profit I now consider loss for the sake of Christ. What is more, I consider everything a loss compared to the surpassing greatness of knowing Christ Jesus my Lord, for whose sake I have lost all things. I consider them rubbish, that I may gain Christ and be found in him, not having a righteousness of my own that comes from the law, but that which is through faith in Christ—the righteousness that comes from God and is by faith" (Philippians 3:7–9).

Paul measured all the things he thought were valuable by the one thing he *knew* to be worthwhile. The comparison was, for him, a no-brainer. Some people are afraid to value a life committed to following Christ because the price seems to be a bit costly.

It may be that what we would give our life for is the truest test of our value system. Arguably, our life is more precious than anything else we possess. If so, what cause, what truth, what experience would you be willing to trade your life for? It's hard to watch people who trade their life on something meaningless or something morally wrong. It is even harder to know that millions in the world today possess nothing that is worth more to them than their life. It helps to know what matters most. As Jesus asked, " 'What good is it for a man to gain the whole world, yet forfeit his soul? Or what can a man give in exchange for his soul?' " (Mark 8:36, 37).

---

1. Jane A. G. Kise, *Finding and Following God's Will* (Bloomington, Minn.: Bethany House, 2005), 48.

Questions for Reflection

1. What popular sayings or bits of cultural wisdom have you adopted into your life?

2. List the things you know and the things you wish you did. Which list was more difficult to make? Why? Did any of your questions or certainties surprise you?

3. When in your life have you felt like you were in a fog and couldn't see which direction you should go? How did you find your way? What sources of insight or guidance were available to you?

4. Sometimes, people's big goals or aspirations distract them from doing the little things they should do today. At other times, people become preoccupied with the little things of everyday life and they never think about the future. Which is the case for you?

5. Which values have you chosen never to compromise?

6. Which guiding proverb is most relevant to you today? Why?

Part II
The Discovery of God's Will

Chapter 3

What He Said

Have you ever pushed on a door when the sign clearly read "pull"? I have. And "shake well before opening" is another of those obvious instructions that I overlook. I can't tell you how many times I approached my elementary school teachers complaining, "This doesn't make any sense to me." Always, without fail, my teachers would reply, "Did you read the instructions?" I would roll my eyes and quietly read the instructions—only to find that the assignment was pretty straightforward.

The search for the will of God begins with the obvious—the Bible. Amazingly, God's Word can pick us apart as would a knife (Hebrews 4:12) but also imbue us with hope in seemingly hopeless moments (Romans 15:4). This Book also claims to be able to reveal the way like a light in the darkness (Psalm 119:105). While it admits openly that it doesn't tell us everything there is to know (John 21:25), it maintains that it provides more than enough for people to believe in and live by (20:30, 31).

One of the most moving stories in the life of Christ occurred when a large number of disciples abandoned Him because His words caused them to cringe. But when Jesus asked His closest disciples if they wanted to leave too, Simon Peter replied, " 'Lord, to whom shall we go? You have the words of eternal life' " (6:68). Paul used the term "word of life," as did John, in reference to the power of Scriptures to change someone's life (Philippians 2:16; 1 John 1:1).

A man who had once been a Christian but who had become a cynic traveled regularly throughout the region of the Baltic Sea. On one of his journeys, he missed the boat that was to take him to his destination, so he caught a ride on a fishing boat that was going the same direction. However, the fishermen took him instead to a tiny island that harbored pirates. Convinced that he would be a dead man when they arrived at the island, the traveler told the fishermen that he was, in fact, a minister. When the boat docked at the island, the fishermen announced that their kidnapped pastor would preach a sermon on Sunday. So, the traveler had no option but to prepare a convincing message for the rabble who would assemble to hear a message from God's Word.

The traveler set about preparing his sermon. When the time came for him to preach to the pirates and other criminals on the island, he made his way to the table they had set up as a pulpit. The pseudo-preacher found one of the few verses he remembered in a Bible that had been placed on the table for him to use in his sermon. Turning to Psalm 58:11, he read, "Verily there is a reward for the righteous: verily he is a God that judgeth in the earth" (KJV). Then he began to elaborate on the rewards of a righteous life and the condemnation of a sinful one. As he unpacked this passage in the Psalms, he remembered other verses that describe forgiveness, the process of repentance, and the need for a new start.

The criminals were broken by the truth of Scripture, and with tears, they made their heartfelt conversion to God that day. And the traveler's own heart began to melt as he observed the impact of God's Word on the pirates. *How could the words of Scripture change this band of reprobates?* he wondered. The next day, the pirates sent him on to his original destination, and as he made his way home, he made a new start with God. The Word of God is powerful.

The Bible doesn't directly answer every question we have about life. It doesn't specifically address every decision we have to make. In fact, the Bible may not speak to many issues that we consider "hot topics." But it's anything but silent about God's will for our lives. I'm not talking about hidden inferences that hint at God's plan for us, but direct, explicit, unmistakable insight into God's will.

I was wandering around the lot of a local auto dealership when a most offensive thing happened. A salesperson approached with a confident smile on his face and introduced himself to me as "the guy who is going to get you the car of your dreams." Then he launched directly into his sales drill, claiming the current sale was so good that there was no way he was letting me leave the lot without a new car because that would be "a crime against humanity." I wanted to smack him. He hadn't even asked my name.

It gets worse. This man then prognosticated about the type of car I was looking for. He said, "You look like an SUV kind of guy! Let me show you one that will blow your mind." (I'm curious as to what an SUV guy looks like.) His arrogance took my breath away, so I played the game with him. I made him work hard for a sale and then revealed to him the true nature of my visit to the dealership: "I'm so glad you showed those cars to me, but I'm really here to buy a fuse for my stereo. Where is the parts department?" I know it was wrong, but I truly enjoyed the look on his face as he pointed to the parts department. I thought to myself, *How dare you claim to know what I want?*

I won't claim to know what you want or need. I don't believe I know all that God has planned for humanity. While such things are personal, God has declared His will in some very specific ways.

Biblical principle #1: God's will is that you receive salvation.

Scripture's primary message about God's will is that He wants you to be saved. Many paths you can take in life may expose you to a myriad of rich experiences, but the one experience God desires most of all is that you make the choice to spend eternity with Him. Here are a few formal declarations of God's will for your life:

- *Chosen from the beginning:* "In him we were also chosen, having been *predestined according to the plan* of him who works out everything in conformity with the purpose of his will, in order that we, who were the first to hope in Christ, might be for the praise of his glory" (Ephesians 1:11, 12; emphasis added).

- *Lost to be found:* " 'What do you think? If a man owns a hundred sheep, and one of them wanders away, will he not leave the ninety-nine on the hills and go to look for the one that wandered off? And if he finds it, I tell you the truth, he is happier about that one sheep than about the ninety-nine that did not wander off. In the same way your Father in heaven is *not willing* that any of these little ones should be lost' " (Matthew 18:12–14; emphasis added).

- *Unwilling that you perish:* "The Lord is not slack concerning His promise, as some count slackness, but is longsuffering toward us, *not willing that any should perish* but that all should come to repentance" (2 Peter 3:9, NKJV; emphasis added).

- *Rescued from evil:* "Grace and peace to you from God our Father and the Lord Jesus Christ, who gave himself for our sins *to rescue us* from the present evil age, according to the will of our God and Father, to whom be glory for ever and ever. Amen" (Galatians 1:3–5; emphasis added).

- *First and foremost—salvation:* "I urge, then, first of all, that requests, prayers, intercession and thanksgiving be made for everyone—for kings and all those in authority, that we may live peaceful and quiet lives in all godliness and holiness. This is good, and pleases God our Savior, *who wants all men to be saved* and to come to a knowledge of the truth" (1 Timothy 2:1–4; emphasis added).

- *Reborn and deployed:* "Then he said: 'The God of our fathers has chosen you *to know his will* and to see the Righteous One and to hear words from his mouth. You will be his witness to all men of what you have seen and heard. And now what are you waiting for? Get up, be baptized and wash your sins away, calling on his name' " (Acts 22:14–16; emphasis added).

It is remarkable how easy it is to major in minors such as "What college should I go to?" when we should be more concerned about the most monumental question, "Where do I spend eternity?" It reminds me of a comical moment on a construction site in 1995. Randy Reid, a construction worker, fell 110 feet and landed on a mound of dirt. Alive but complaining of pain in his back, he lay still until help came. And when the paramedics arrived and placed him on a backboard, Randy said, "Please don't drop me."

Sometimes we can be like Randy: God saves us from the big fall, but we become skittish about the three-foot drop. It may be that we'll see more clearly the answers to the concerns we have about our minor plans when we view them against the backdrop of salvation's peace.

What else is there to say? When people ask, "What does God want for my life?" the answer is always, "You! He wants you." Choose your career prayerfully and thoughtfully. But God is more interested in your salvation than in whether you become a doctor or a computer programmer. While your learning *the hard way* may not be *His way*, God would rather have you bumped and bruised by life than not have you at all.

In a state penitentiary, I listened to a convicted felon describe his journey to receiving Christ as his Savior from sin. He said that God would rather he be sitting in jail clinging fully to the grace of Christ than living a successful, self-sufficient life without God. Does God really care whether we go to school in Texas or Michigan if where we spend eternity is in serious question? Clearly, God wants you to receive the free gift of salvation more than anything else.

Biblical principle #2: God's will is that we grow.

The natural world has many wonders, but its most basic feature is that everything that is alive grows, develops, and changes over time. Unquestionably, personal transformation ranks high on God's wish list. Some might struggle with this point, thinking that the idea of growth contradicts the concept of grace. But our growth, no matter how slow or inconsistent, doesn't cancel the free gift of God's mercy. With this truth firmly in place, we can examine the many passages that convey how deep God's desire is that we grow. Here are three of them:

- *Mature and confident:* "Epaphras, who is one of you and a servant of Christ Jesus, sends greetings. He is always wrestling in prayer for you, that you may stand firm in all *the will of God, mature and fully assured*" (Colossians 4:12; emphasis added).

- *Fruit-bearing believers:* "Since the day we heard about you, we have not stopped praying for you and asking God to fill you with the knowledge of *his will* through all spiritual wisdom and understanding. And we pray this in order that you may live a life worthy of the Lord and may please him in every way: *bearing fruit in every good work*, growing in the knowledge of God, being strengthened with all power according to his glorious might so that you may have great endurance and patience, and joyfully giving thanks to the Father, who has qualified you to share in the inheritance of the saints in the kingdom of light" (1:9–12; emphasis added).

- *Sanctified:* "*It is God's will that you should be sanctified* [set apart for a special purpose]: that you should avoid sexual immorality; that each of you should learn to control his own body in a way that is holy and honorable, not in passionate lust like the heathen, who do not know God; and that in this matter no one should wrong his brother or take advantage of him" (1 Thessalonians 4:3–6; emphasis added).

As a child, I watched the tangerine tree in my yard grow to monstrous proportions. Not only did our citrus tree grow in size, but the crop of fruit that it produced also overwhelmed my family and our friends. My pride in the tree swelled from season to season—so much so that I thought the skill of growing fruit trees was simply genetic; I couldn't lose.

When I grew up and the time came for me to plant my own fruit trees in my very own backyard, I picked out a tangerine tree to repeat the success of my childhood. I did everything to the soil that I had been taught to do—I cultivated, fertilized, mulched, protected, and prayed. After I planted the tree, I continued the rituals week after week. I also spoke kindly and gently to the tree as I worked in the yard, and on one occasion, I even sang to it. But the tree failed to grow.

So, my patience ran out, and I began to scorn the defenseless citrus tree. "Useless runt weed! What's the matter with you?" I chided it. "Every other tree in the yard is doing just fine. You are turning out to be such a disappointment!"

One day, I was raking some leaves in the yard near the puny tangerine tree when my rake got stuck on a tag at its base. I reached down to unhook the prongs of the rake and discovered that the tag identifying the tree was still attached. To my dismay, I read, "Tangerine (Dwarf)."

I tried to take back all the horrible things I said. I looked at the little tree and apologized saying, "I'm so sorry! I didn't realize you were never meant to grow much."

Not so with you and me. According to Christ, we are destined to change into His likeness. And the transformation doesn't take place in some moment in the future but little by little each day.

Biblical principle #3: God's will is that we be filled with His Spirit.

Being "filled with the Spirit" was for me just another overdone Christian cliché until I met Sarah. She was a communications major who worked with junior high students and had a gift for creative expressions of biblical truths. Standing before a restless group of eager teens with a pitcher of clear water and a clear glass half filled with mud, she said, "Some of you have asked me privately, 'How do we get God to help us get rid of the bad stuff in our lives?' Well, maybe this demonstration will help you." Sarah held up the glass of mud and said, "This is you. You have stuff in your life you want to get rid of to make room for God, right?"

Sarah continued, "The only way I know how to get rid of the mud in the glass is to use water. Now, you can pour a little water in at a time, and this is what you get." The glass of mud filled up with, well, more mud. "Or," she said, "you can flush the mud out with water, like this." She began to pour a steady stream of clean water into the glass, and little by little, the water flushed the mud out. The students did the rest of the work by discussing the significance of the lesson. As one of them stated, "It's not enough to add a little water every once in a while. You have to flush it out with a lot."

Consider what Paul says about God's will for us: "Do not be foolish, but *understand what the Lord's will is*. Do not get drunk on wine, which leads to debauchery. Instead, *be filled with the Spirit*. Speak to one another with psalms, hymns and spiritual songs. Sing and make music in your heart to the Lord, always giving thanks to God the Father for everything, in the name of our Lord Jesus Christ. Submit to one another out of reverence for Christ" (Ephesians 5:17–21; emphasis added).

Kyle, a student of mine, visited a charismatic church service as part of an assignment. He told me that he was taken aback when someone questioned him abruptly as to whether he had "received the Spirit" yet. He said, "I felt like something was wrong with me because I wasn't rolling in the aisle or speaking in tongues." What Paul says about being "filled with the Spirit" is much different. He focused on our worship being something that begins "in our hearts."

What does God really want? According to this portion of Scripture, God wants us to have the kind of indwelling experience that makes our conversations full of insight and encouragement. He wants us to become people who can be thankful in any circumstance, good or bad. He wants us to be so filled with the Spirit of Christ that we'll be humble enough to submit to others in the body of Christ. In order to be able to live together in community, we need to be willing to learn from each other.

Biblical principle #4: God's will is that we work for others with a servant's heart.

In light of the fact that most of us will ultimately spend a significant portion of our week at work, God's plan is that we use that time well by being deliberate about our work ethic. While the following biblical passage is directed at those who were servants to others, the principle of humble service applies to every sector of the working world. Paul calls believers to leverage their influence in the workplace by treating their supervisors with genuine respect and kindness. "Slaves, obey your earthly masters with respect and fear, and with sincerity of heart, just as you would obey Christ. Obey them not only to win their favor when their eye is on you, but like slaves of Christ, *doing the will of God from your heart*. Serve wholeheartedly, as if you were serving the Lord, not men, because you know that the Lord will reward everyone for whatever good he does, whether he is slave or free" (Ephesians 6:5–8; emphasis added).

Employers long to have employees who are loyal, selfless, and sincere. Being an employee of that caliber is part of God's will for our lives. You might remember the story of Joseph and how God could use him because Joseph was willing to be a servant—and, when it was time, a leader. Bookstores are filled with resources that preach the concept of servant leadership. The core concept of most of these books is that our character—who we are—is what influences others in one direction or another. God has a plan for your life, and it includes the 40 percent of each day that you spend at work or school.

Biblical principle #5: God's will is that we quiet the critics with acts of goodness.

If there was ever an aspect of God's will that I'm tempted to ignore, it is that God wants us to say less and do more. This principle applies to everything from evangelism to the politics of the boardroom. Admittedly, I would rather tell "ignorant people" to kindly refrain from their mindless commentary (not necessarily in those terms, however). But catch the wisdom in God's way of dealing with people who annoy us: "It is God's will that by doing good you should silence the ignorant talk of foolish men" (1 Peter 2:15).

Practice this principle. Add it to your list of "God's will for my life," and discover how goodness expressed in tangible acts of kindness relieves the frustration posed by annoying people and fills your heart with confidence and peace. Instead of well-rehearsed speeches meant to cut down the people who frustrate you, compassion for them will emerge from your heart. (Am I the only one out there who rehearses telling someone off?)

Kevin was drawing near the end of his student teaching assignment—and with each day that passed, he was coming closer to thumping one particular student for his disruptive behavior. Even the students in class were sick of the constant interruptions and ridiculous questions. Kevin took the advice of a seasoned teacher (and of Peter) and took the sassy young man to lunch, then to a ball game, and later invited him to help with a service project. Two things eventually happened: The student sensed Kevin's kindness and lightened up on the annoying behavior a little. And Kevin's kindness fostered within him a genuine affinity for the student, and he became less easily annoyed. Investing our heart and energy in people develops our love for them.

Biblical principle #6: God's will for us is an abundant life.

Think of someone in your life who comes close to personifying the qualities revealed in this passage: "Be joyful always; pray continually; give thanks in all circumstances, for *this is God's will for you in Christ Jesus*" (1 Thessalonians 5:16–18; emphasis added).

Some people try to attract others to following Christ by saying, "Christianity can be fun!" But I don't hear Christ ever saying, "Follow Me—it's fun!" Rather, I hear the opposite:

- You will be misunderstood.
- People will hate you.
- Some will try to harm you, thinking they are doing God a favor.
- You are to be a servant, not the star of the show.
- You will have no place to lay your head.

In fact, check out the Beatitudes and see how much fun it is to be subjects of the kingdom of God. Yet, an appropriate translation of the recurring word *blessed* is "happy." Following Christ is an exciting, meaningful, and rewarding experience that is rich in purpose—and at times, it can even be extremely fun. John equates the experience with the word "life" (1 John 5:11). But this life also includes pain, frustration, and disappointment. Often, when Paul was writing things like "be joyful" and "give thanks in all circumstances," he was writing from a prison cell. That's not fun—but it is full. Paul continues to reveal the secret of such joy by challenging believers to "pray continually." Regular conversation with God creates a soul strength that enables us to endure. Frankly, people like that are a treasure to be around. And like the previous passages, this appeal is God's will for your life.

The question you might ask yourself at this point is, Do you know what you should do today to live God's will for your life? If you were to devote yourself to these attitudes and activities on a regular basis, do you really think your wheels would be spinning about what the future may or may not hold? Would you not have enough to do today?

Think about people you know who live this way. Do they wander around confused with no clue what to do? The people I know who want to live God's will don't worry about the future or whether they are in the "right place at the right time." Their lives are full of grace and deep with meaning and covered with contentment.

You may want to know what tomorrow holds. But ultimately, God wants you to know Him so that when tomorrow comes, you'll already know all you need to know. As 1 John 5:20 puts it, "We know also that the Son of God has come and has given us understanding, so that we may know him who is true."

Biblical principle #7: God's will is something we discover experientially.

Jesus said, " 'If anyone chooses to do God's will, he will find out whether my teaching comes from God or whether I speak on my own' " (John 7:17, 18). Clarity comes in the aftermath of a commitment. Notice how Paul puts it: "Do not conform any longer to the pattern of this world, but be transformed by the renewing of your mind. *Then* you will be able to test and approve what God's will is—his good, pleasing and perfect will" (Romans 12:2; emphasis added).

One quagmire that traps people in search of God's will is the notion that it is something to know. They assume that God reveals the plan for our lives and we can then choose whether we want to participate or go another direction. However, Ray Pritchard points out that "God ordinarily will not show you His will in order for you to consider it."[1] Essentially, God reveals His will to those who are willing to do it.

I think God operates this way for a couple of reasons. First, it may be that God doesn't reveal the future to us because we wouldn't believe it if we saw it. God's plans for us are too great—well beyond anything we could dream up on our own. If God were to show us where we'll be ten years from now, it's likely that we'd shake our heads and say "No way." Second, God may hold back on showing us the whole picture because He knows that if He were to do that, we might not cling to Him daily—and more than achieving the perfect life, He longs for us to cling to Him with perfect trust.

When the topic of God's will comes up in Scripture, it often appears as something to be done rather than something to be known or understood. *Doing* God's will is so tied to *knowing* God's will that it seems the chicken-and-egg dynamic is at play. But remember the words contained in the Lord's Prayer, "Thy kingdom come, thy will be done on earth as it is in heaven." Those who are willing to do God's will no matter what will discover and know it. Furthermore, those who do God's will are intimately acquainted with God's plan from personal experience. Consider just a few samples from Scripture on doing God's will.

- " 'I said, "Here I am—it is written about me in the scroll—I have come *to do your will*, O God" ' " (Hebrews 10:7; emphasis added).

- " 'Not everyone who says to me, "Lord, Lord," will enter the kingdom of heaven, but *only he who does the will of my Father* who is in heaven' " (Matthew 7:21; emphasis added).

- " 'Whoever *does the will of my Father* in heaven is my brother and sister and mother' " (12:50; emphasis added).

- " 'I desire to *do your will*, O my God; your law is within my heart' " (Psalm 40:8; emphasis added).

- "You need to persevere so that when you have *done the will of God*, you will receive what he has promised" (Hebrews 10:36; emphasis added).

- "May the God of peace, who through the blood of the eternal covenant brought back from the dead our Lord Jesus, that great Shepherd of the sheep, equip you with everything good for *doing his will*, and may he work in us what is pleasing to him, through Jesus Christ, to whom be glory for ever and ever. Amen" (13:20, 21; emphasis added).

- "This world is fading away, along with everything that people crave. But anyone who does what pleases *God* will live forever" (1 John 2:17, NLT; emphasis added).

Let's review: First, while many things about the future remain undis-closed, God clearly conveys His ultimate will for us in His Word. We may want to know if our destiny includes being a doctor or a dressmaker, whether we will live in New Guinea or New Jersey, but God wants us to be saved, transformed, and living the abundant life—the Bible is clear on that! Second, God has revealed enough for us to choose His will and therefore choose His way. Our part is to choose to embrace His plan without seeing all of it—that's called faith. And third, ultimately, we gain an intimate knowledge of God's guiding ways as we walk with Him by doing His will. This discovery is experiential as well as intellectual.

One final word on God's Word. Seeking guidance from Scripture will never be as engaging as becoming absorbed in a novel or watching a movie. While the Bible is an obvious place to look for guidance, many are unsatisfied when it doesn't leap out and lead them through the big decisions of life. But the Bible wasn't written to be prescriptive in the way a counselor or a consultant would offer guidance. It's a confluence of stories, history, letters, and liturgy as well as prophetic instruction. It is ancient, and yet its message to humanity is timeless. It is the inspired Word of God. But its connection to our world today requires a bit of earnest study. We need to be seekers to understand it. If we want the Bible to help us find God's will, then we must integrate its message into our life. In order even to understand it, we need to be willing to do what it says. It may seem outrageous, but God's Word guides us when we give ourselves wholly to its ultimate claim.

One day I served my students all a cup of hot water and a tea bag. I pa-tronized them a bit by saying, "Today, I'm going to teach you how to make a cup of tea." When they'd stopped rolling their eyes, I commenced with the instructions, "First, dip your tea bag in the water until I say 'Stop.' "

When everyone's bag had been in the water for three seconds, I said, "OK, that's enough. Take your tea bags out."

The class sputtered with random bursts of disapproval.

"What's wrong?" I chided them. "Taste your tea!"

Of course, the water in their cups was barely colored and had almost no taste.

I invited the students to put their tea bags back in the water, and this time I waited about thirty seconds. Then I said, "How does it taste now?" Lemon. Mint. Orange Spice. There was flavor.

The point: God's Word offers us more guidance when we get into it than when we merely consult it.[2]

1. Ray Pritchard, *The Road Best Traveled: Knowing God's Will for Your Life* (Wheaton, Ill.: Crossway Books, 1995), 44.

2. The appendix contains an inductive guide to Bible study from the Go Figure series by Troy Fitzgerald.

Questions for Reflection

1. Is it your experience that while most people would agree that God guides us through His Word, they tend to look for a more dynamic way of being led? What avenues of God's guidance other than Scripture have you sought?

2. Regarding the decisions you face today, does it seem like the Bible is eminently relevant or somewhat removed from your life?

3. This chapter discusses the explicit will of God as it emerges from the pages of Scripture. What do you think is God's most pressing desire for you today? If God were to write a wish list, what do you think would be His foremost wish?

4. If you were to avail yourself daily of God's will as He has clearly revealed it in His Word, you wouldn't struggle with uncertainty or doubt about the day-to-day decisions of life. Do you agree or disagree with the preceding statement? Why?

5. This chapter says that God's will is something we *do* more than something we *know*. Has this been true in your experience? In what way is God's will something we learn experientially? What examples can you share from your own journey?

6. Has God revealed enough of His will for you to give yourself completely to Him?

7. What passages or stories from Scripture in this chapter were especially meaningful to you? Why?

Chapter 4

God's Will vs. Your Will

Discovering God's will is only part of the journey. Choosing God's way versus our way stirs up another conundrum.

Of all the muscles my oldest son, Cameron, can flex, his will is most impressive. As we were playing outside on a sunny summer afternoon, we noticed the cat across the street lying in the grass, lazily playing with a toy. When we looked closer, it became clear that the cat's toy of the day was a baby rabbit. The bunny, frozen with fear in a tight ball in front of the cat, shivered in the warm sun. The wet marks on the bunny's fur made it clear that the cat had been "playing" with it for a while. The scene was awful.

The little suburban hunter hissed at us in outrage when we approached. Cameron was outraged too. Actually, outrage is a gross understatement of what he was feeling. I tried to guide him away from the scene, telling him there was nothing we could do for the bunny. He refused to accept my assessment of the situation and turned back to watch the cat. I continued to instruct him about the danger of attempting a rescue, saying, "That cat will scratch you up if you try and rescue that bunny, Cameron."

Now, we cry different kinds of tears: tears of sorrow, tears of joy, and even tears when we are confused and don't know what to do. But the tears that filled my son's eyes that day were tears of rage. "I'm going to get that bunny," he said adamantly.

"Oh no you aren't!" I replied, making sure he heard my directive. "I'm not losing my firstborn to a silly cat. Cameron, do not disobey me. I mean it."

I placed my hand on his shoulder to guide him back home. As he walked with me, I could feel his whole body resisting. When we had crossed the street, he ducked under my protective arm and bolted back to the scene in deliberate defiance of my instructions. Even as I yelled, "Cameron, stop," all I could do was stare in disbelief.

Cameron raced across the street right up to the cat, and without hesitation or hint of fear, scooped up the tiny bunny in his little hands. The glee in his eyes squeezed the remaining tears down his cheeks as he ran back to our house. I wondered how I would ever discipline him for disobeying me—I could just imagine all heaven putting me on notice for scolding him for such a compassionate act of grace. As my son sat in the grass feeding little bits of pink clover to his friend, I reflected on the strength of the human will.

I believe some people are psychologically wired to be strong-willed, while others are inclined to be more laid back about getting their way. Whether the quality is inherent or fostered by upbringing (or perhaps both), people can use willpower for good or for evil. My friend Glenn taught me that our apparent weaknesses are often strengths carried to excess. People who might come off as domineering could simply be strong leaders with too much time on their hands. Some possess the quality of meekness; without healthy boundaries, they become doormats instead of doorways of God's grace to others. Those who are described as stubborn may simply have an overdeveloped grip on their will. Whether you possess a strong will or you are more compliant, your will needs to be aligned with God's will as you learn to live God's plan for your life.

The most endearing quality of strong-willed people is their ability to endure adversity for the sake of principle. When I was young, my father was a serious drinker. I don't remember a whole lot about my feelings about the matter now, but I think I mentioned to him that I didn't like the way he consumed alcohol. I remember coming in the door from school one afternoon and seeing my dad sitting quietly in the living room with a book in his lap. That was weird; I'd never seen my dad read. Even more strange was the absence of the bar that occupied the corner of the family room. It was gone. I looked outside and found that this large piece of party furniture had been emptied and set beside the house. I wondered, *What happened to my father?* The short side of the longer story is that he had found Christ. My dad has never had a drink since that moment.

How is it that he could just stop drinking? Certainly, God had given him something new to live for. But alcohol is a drug—an addictive substance that requires willpower to quit. Dad has always been able to set his mind on something and follow through—whether it is a project, hard work, or making sacrifices. He sticks to his principles and rarely flinches in the face of adversity. Perhaps those who are strong-willed have a harder time than others becoming convinced that they need to change direction, but when they finally experience such a conviction, they follow through like champions. Likewise, those who tend to yield more readily might easily sense a need for change but struggle to follow through when the going gets tough. Ultimately, no matter where we are at on the personality spectrum, the road to God's plan for our life runs right through our will.

To get a handle on God's will, we need to face up to the competition. But if you are thinking the enemy is a host of supernatural forces with names like "Satan" or "Devil" or "Evil One," then you may want to sit down. On the journey to discovering God's will for your life, *you* will get in the way more often than anyone else will. Lucifer might be the poster boy for selfishness and the chief architect of evil, but God created his creatures with the ability to choose, which makes following God's guidance an issue of your will.

In *Steps to Christ*, Ellen White penned, "The warfare against self is the greatest battle that was ever fought. The yielding of self, surrendering all to the will of God, requires a struggle; but the soul must submit to God before it can be renewed in holiness."[1] Paul wrote of this battle in Romans, confessing, "I do not understand my own actions. For I do not do what I want, but I do the very thing I hate" (Romans 7:15, ESV). Paul not only sounds conflicted but also seems to be in despair about this war that rages within his own heart: "I know that nothing good dwells in me, that is, in my flesh. For I have the desire to do what is right, but not the ability to carry it out" (verse 18, ESV). We can't do even the things *we* want to do, not to mention the things that God wants us to do. So, the war of the wills rages within every human being, and the result is never a tie. Some side always wins, and the other loses.

The fall of Lucifer involved the struggle between the rule of self and the rule of God in the honored angel's heart. This war continued in Adam and Eve, and it is a reality in everyone born of a woman from Eden to this moment. *All* temptation finds its center in a struggle between our will and God's will. Even the temptations Jesus faced were about choosing another way (self) over God's way (sacrifice).

William Dembski cited a prayer prayed by Homer Simpson (yes, the cartoon character) that touches on what people pray for and whether they expect answers. Homer's wife tries to interrupt the prayer with news that she is pregnant with their third child. " 'Can't talk now—praying,' [Homer] interrupts. 'Dear Lord, the gods have been good to me and I am thankful. For the first time in my life, everything is absolutely perfect the way it is. So here's the deal: you freeze everything as it is and I won't ask for anything more. If that is okay, please give me absolutely no sign. [pause] Okay, deal. In gratitude, I present to you this offering of cookies and milk. If you want me to eat them for you, please give me no sign. [pause] Thy will be done.' "[2]

Consider the prayers we tend to pray: Prayers for protection. Prayers for forgiveness. Prayers to bless the food. Prayers for the people we love to experience grace. Prayers for ourselves to change a specific behavior or attitude. The precious little book *Children's Letters to God* contains a prayer that a child wrote rather glibly, " 'Thanks for the baby brother, but what I asked for was a puppy.' "[3] But the prayer we find hardest to pray is the prayer Jesus prayed in Gethsemane.

"Your will be done."

Today, God's will is not done on earth as it is in heaven, which makes the Lord's Prayer especially relevant. But the other Lord's prayer, the prayer Christ prayed in Gethsemane, might be the most difficult prayer we will ever pray. Those who think praying "Your will be done" is a cop-out or an act of cowardice need to take another look. No one will ever make a more heroic response to a greater challenge than Christ did when He prayed for God's will to be done. Consider the battle as portrayed in *The Desire of Ages*:

> The awful moment had come—that moment which was to decide the destiny of the world. The fate of humanity trembled in the balance. Christ might even now refuse to drink the cup apportioned to guilty man. It was not yet too late. He might wipe the bloody sweat from His brow, and leave man to perish in his iniquity. He might say, Let the transgressor receive the penalty of his sin, and I will go back to My Father. Will the Son of God drink the bitter cup of humiliation and agony? Will the in-

nocent suffer the consequences of the curse of sin, to save the guilty? The words fall tremblingly from the pale lips of Jesus, "O My Father, if this cup may not pass away from Me, except I drink it, Thy will be done."

Three times has He uttered that prayer. Three times has humanity shrunk from the last, crowning sacrifice. But now the history of the human race comes up before the world's Redeemer. He sees that the transgressors of the law, if left to themselves, must perish. He sees the helplessness of man. He sees the power of sin. The woes and lamentations of a doomed world rise before Him. He beholds its impending fate, and His decision is made. He will save man at any cost to Himself. He accepts His baptism of blood, that through Him perishing millions may gain everlasting life. He has left the courts of heaven, where all is purity, happiness, and glory, to save the one lost sheep, the one world that has fallen by transgression. And He will not turn from His mission. He will become the propitiation of a race that has willed to sin. His prayer now breathes only submission: "If this cup may not pass away from Me, except I drink it, Thy will be done."[4]

When Jesus entered the Garden of Gethsemane, He had a decision to make about God's will. The choice was clear. There was no ambiguity about whether or not Calvary was God's will for Him. He had come to earth and lived here thirty-three years in order to die, and He knew it. Following through with God's plan meant separation from His Father—the second death. He wasn't confused about His options. He didn't need more information or contingency plans. What He needed was comfort. He needed courage. He needed to surrender His will and embrace His purpose as the Sin Bearer. The choice was not hard to understand—it was hard to do. So He prayed, " 'Father, if you are willing, take this cup from me; yet not my will, but yours be done' " (Luke 22:42).

Know this: To pray "Your will be done" is not a timid plea or retreat; it's a war cry like no other in the universe. God's will on earth flies in the face of all that is unjust and evil. To pray that prayer is to make the consummate protest against selfish living and to take a courageous stand for God's kingdom to have indisputable rule in our hearts. About this prayer, Ray Pritchard asserts, "They are fighting words, words that rebel against everything that is evil and wrong on Planet Earth. . . . To pray, 'Your will be done' is an act of God-ordained rebellion! This is not a prayer for the weak or the timid. This prayer is for trouble makers and rabble-rousers."[5]

One of my students shared with me his resistance to being open to God's leading in his life. He confessed, "I'm not sure I want to go there. God has kind of a strange track record of always leading people out of their comfort zone." Then, smiling, he admitted, "I have really grown accustomed to my comfort zone. It's pretty comfortable."

My response to his honest admission was, "Yeah, it's obviously comfortable. But is it safe?"

A year later, this guy caught me on my way to class, informing me that he had just returned from spending a year abroad as a Bible teacher. He evidently made a last-minute decision to travel to the other side of the world and teach Bible to high school students.

He said he had spent two days in agonizing, heartfelt prayer before he could choke out the words, "Not my will, but Yours be done." And he said, "I was right; God does lead you out of your comfort zone. And you were right, as well. You are safe only when you live according to God's will."

Have you ever wondered why praying that prayer is difficult? Let's examine some obstacles that get in the way of our praying this prayer, and then let's consider how to pray this prayer and actually mean it.

Obstacle #1: Freedom

The things that wrinkle our readiness to do God's will may grow out of our assumptions about freedom. Surrendering our plans and our desires is not only unnatural, it's also un-American. Deep in the heart of Western thinking is a sense of entitlement to certain liberties. We think of freedom as "the absence of external restraint and the protection—as well as the expansion—of personal rights."[6] But the Gospels indicate that we obtain the freedom that Jesus offers only by submitting to Him as one of His disciples. He said, " 'If you hold to my teaching, you are really my disciples. Then you will know the truth, and the truth will set you free' " (John 8:31, 32). He hinted at a distinction between His freedom and any other kind when He said, " 'If the Son sets you free, you will be free indeed' " (verse 36). In other words, only when Jesus sets you free do you experience true freedom.

Perhaps the following story will illustrate the difference between being "free" and what Christ meant by being "free indeed." For one reason or another, numerous people—the homeless, the deranged, the broken, the cast outs, the has-beens, the addicts, the mindless, the misfits—have made their dwelling in the sewers below New York City. Jennifer Toth, a reporter, chose to live among them for a while. In her book *The Mole People*, she cites an interchange with a man who gave an interview in exchange for a free lunch.

This man, Flacko, a would-be leader underground, said, " 'If I was in charge I'd put up a big sign on the platform saying, "C'mon down! Everyone welcome! Come live free—rent-free, tax-free, independent, free like Mandela!" When he stops smiling, he turns earnest and leans over our table in the Chinese restaurant. . . . 'If you write this book,' he says, 'you tell them the tunnels rob you of your life. No one should come down here. . . . Everyone down here knows it. They won't say it, but they know it.' "[7]

Is it possible that the great paradox of the Christian life is that we are truly free only when we willingly surrender our lives to God?

Obstacle #2: Control

Perhaps you have noticed the human need for control when you've been a passenger in a car. My wife and I are both relatively moderate in our driving, yet when I'm driving, she perceives my jerks and twists and changes in speed as different from what she does when she's driving. (Admittedly, I do the same thing.) Riding is an entirely different experience than driving. And the experience of surrendering control of our life to God is keenly similar.

Western culture tends to value the quality of self-reliance. Containing lines such as "It's my life," "Like Frankie said, / 'I did it my way,' " and "I just wanna live while I'm alive," Bon Jovi's hit song "Its My Life" portrays the popular notion that we own our lives and make our dreams come true. Decisive, self-determining people rise to the top of our list of "most successful humans." Simply stated, we admire those who know where they are going and how to get there. On the other hand, college students who are "undecided" about their major may feel self-conscious about their status in contrast to those who have clearly mapped out the future. The claim, "If I want something bad enough, I will get it," might seem a bit precocious, but such a commitment to personal goals stirs a quiet admiration from the baser side of our humanity.

Seeking this kind of control, though, flies in the face of praying, "Thy will be done." We find it hard to pray this prayer because doing so means we're essentially giving up control of our life. Such a prayer surrenders the quest for selfish trophies; it applies full concentration to another's endeavors. From a worldly perspective, it's a roadblock.

However, it doesn't make sense that we, who didn't create the world or construct a master plan to save the human race, would feel safer in our own hands than in God's. How the angels must marvel at us as we ferociously plan and protect ourselves with all of our human resources. In light of the truth that God is good and knows the future, the fact that we wrest the wheel of our life away from Him is a serious conundrum.

Obstacle #3: Doubt

Another reason we struggle to submit to God's will when it differs from our own is that deep down inside we doubt that God wants what is best for us. It may sound like heresy at first, but let me explain. Consider the millions and millions of earnest, honest, heartfelt prayers that have called on God to do something good when something obviously bad was taking place. The Holocaust. Slavery in the South. Starvation in India. Genocide in Africa. Rape. Abuse. Murder. Loneliness. Do the math: If God is in control and God is a God of love, why does everything seem to be out of control? We don't want to let what we don't know confuse us about what we do know. But what should we do with our unanswered questions about God's inaction? I think they bother us, but we don't ever say so because it sounds irreverent. Maybe one of the reasons we hold back on asking God to have His way with us is that we wonder if God would put us in circumstances that we would never choose for ourselves.

If someone asks, "Hey, Troy, can you do me a favor?" I'd likely respond, "Well, what do you have in mind?" I'd want to know what the favor is before I say yes. Actually, how I respond would depend on who is asking. If my mom were to ask me for a favor, I'd say, "Yeah, Mom, what is it?" I'd say that because I'm confident that my mother is loving and good and would never seek to harm me. I'd have very little fear about responding to her request.

We respond differently to God because we've seen what He's done with people who say, "Yes, God, whatever You want." The truth is that saying yes to God is scary. We feel we know what is best for us, and we define the good life as the absence of pain and the presence of prosperity. But in Christ's case, God said the good life was Calvary. For Job, it was target practice for Satan. For some Christians, it was an arena full of lions. We'll tackle the logistics of adversity in the next chapter, but for now, let's delve deeper into the conflict between what we think is best for us and what we fear God thinks is best for us.

The hard, honest truth is that we must at some point trust that God's ways are not just different from our ways, but His ways are higher and better—even the best way imaginable. Ellen White said, "Would that all who have not chosen Christ might realize that He has something vastly better to offer them than they are seeking for themselves. Man is doing the greatest injury and injustice to his own soul when he thinks and acts contrary to the will of God."[8]

To illustrate this principle, I placed on my classroom table ten gift bags filled with treasures. All the bags were shiny and appealing, but nine of the bags contained relatively worthless items, such as rocks, pieces of wood, and sand. I had loaded the tenth bag with cookies, candy, and ice-cream gift certificates. Then I said that the last person who entered class could either choose one of the bags and be the sole owner of the contents, or this person could choose someone he or she trusted to do the choosing.

Janet came to class late, so she became the "volunteer." She ruminated on her dilemma for a few moments, and then she asked me, the teacher who had placed the items in the bags, to choose for her. Of course, I picked the bag full of good things for her.

I discussed with the class the implications of this exercise for our relationship with God. Clearly, the ideal criteria for selecting someone to do the choosing would be (1) choose someone who knows which bag held the treats, and (2) choose someone whom you trust to choose well for you. The bottom line is, Does God know what is best for us, and can we trust Him to lead us in the best way?

It's a process.

Choosing God's will over our own isn't a one-time event or experience. It's a process—a process of surrender. In fact, I'm not sure the surrender of our will ever feels totally complete—perhaps because life is so complex. We make decisions about so many things without even thinking about God's will.

The process of surrender typically begins with a conversation with God about the nature of His will and how it might differ from ours. The next stage involves cooperating with God, beginning with our initiative and action. The process culminates in our will and God's will becoming one. Consider some of the steps to praying "not my will, but Yours be done."

Step #1: Conversation

Sometimes we talk around God, as though He's not even in the room. Some of the more useless diatribes about God and His guidance occur with all the right ideas but with the wrong person. I remember feeling horrible about a careless word I said that hurt a friend. I think I apologized for the callous word to ten people before someone said, "Why don't you tell the person you hurt how sorry you are?" To take the first step toward choosing God's will, we need to have a conversation with God Himself. It's perfectly OK to request, like Jesus, "If it is possible, let this cup pass from me." Honesty begets genuine commitment. The more honest and upfront we are with God, the deeper, more complete faith in His guiding ways we'll find ourselves experiencing.

Remember that conversations are a two-way street, and in the absence of an epiphany or a burning bush, listen to God's Word about His will for your life. In Hebrews, the apostle wrote, "In the past God spoke to our forefathers through the prophets at many times and in various ways, but in these last days he has spoken to us by his Son, whom he appointed heir of all things, and through whom he made the universe" (Hebrews 1:1, 2). Whenever I return to the life of Christ, I find an endless flow of examples to follow, insight to apply, challenges to embrace, and choices to make. If you're waiting for God to call you on your cell phone, get over it. He has spoken so perfectly in the flesh and blood of His Son that no other media can compare.

I'm not a journaler. But during a season of serious disorientation, I decided to write my thoughts, prayers, and questions to God in a journal and then scan the pages of a red-letter-edition Bible and write the things Jesus said that seemed to be speaking to my heart. That journal, filled with tears and triumphant passages from my life and the words of Christ, became an anchoring rock in my spiritual journey.

Step #2: Cooperation

In the absence of a specific itinerary for your life or a crystal ball that tells all, those who converse with God about His will need to take some initiative. The Bible says, "By faith Abraham, when called to go to a place he would later receive as his inheritance, obeyed and went, even though he did not know where he was going" (Hebrews 11:8). No specific direction. No road map. But as Abraham took the initiative to pick up his left foot and then his right foot, he was beginning to cooperate with God. While God rarely reveals His will for people to consider, He often guides those who cooperate with Him step by step. Initiative and action. Consider a few passages from the pros who learned what it means to cooperate with God in a give-and-take relationship.

- Paul declared, "As you have always obeyed—not only in my presence, but now much more in my absence—continue to work out your salvation with fear and trembling, for it is God who works in you to will and to act according to his good purpose" (Philippians 2:12, 13).

- And to the church of Galatia, Paul asserted, "Those who belong to Christ Jesus have crucified the sinful nature with its passions and desires. Since we live by the Spirit, let us keep in step with the Spirit" (Galatians 5:24, 25).

- Peter claimed, "His divine power has given us everything we need for life and godliness through our knowledge of him who called us by his own glory and goodness. . . . For this very reason, make every effort to add to your faith goodness; and to goodness, knowledge" (2 Peter 1:3, 5).

- David, singer, songwriter, and king of Israel, pleaded with God, "Teach me to do your will, for you are my God; may your good Spirit lead me on level ground" (Psalm 143:10).

Cooperating with God calls for active participation in spiritual matters. Take the initiative to serve others in a tangible way. Start a small-group Bible study. Visit and care for the widows and orphans. Begin with the things God has clearly posited in Scripture and see what happens. As you faithfully engage in activities that deepen your commitment to God, His will becomes clearer and clearer.

Step #3: Culmination
This step is more of a byproduct of the first two, but it is important to recognize that God's goal is that our will and His come together as

one—unlikely as that may seem. It has been said that "obedience is the alignment of our will to God's." Christ referred to the confluence of our will with God's in His prayer recorded in John 17. He said, " 'I in them and you in me. May they be brought to complete unity to let the world know that you sent me and have loved them even as you have loved me' " (verse 23). In 1 John, the apostle whom Jesus loved wrote, "This is love for God: to obey his commands. And his commands are not burdensome" (5:3). As we enter into a conversation with Jesus about His will for our life and as we actively cooperate with Him through action, His will is fused into our hearts in a rich, intimate union.

Chuck Swindoll explained why doing God's will is often a complicated, mysterious journey: "Because we don't know where He is taking us, we must bend our will to His—and most of us are not all that excited about bending. We'd much prefer resisting. That's why the Christian life is often a struggle. I don't mean that it's a constant marathon of misery. It's just a struggle between our will and His."[9]

Remember, God doesn't reveal His will so we can consider it—He reveals it when we choose to obey it. Only those who bend and conform like clay will find joy in being shaped by God's guiding hand. As I've noted repeatedly, the prayer we'll find most difficult to pray is for God's will to be done in place of ours.

We understand many aspects of God's character better when we become parents: Unconditional love. Selflessness. Even a willingness to die in place of our children if need be. However, when I think of the goals and plans I have for my kids, I never include suffering, failure, or loss. I just can't bring myself to see them broken by life. I think we find it hard to pray "Thy will be done" because we've watched God deliberately walk His children right through hell purposefully, and sometimes without explanation or apology. To us, it doesn't ever seem like the best way. I can quite easily admit that God's ways are not my ways, but I struggle to believe that they are better. But I should know better.

Some think that surrendering their will to God means forfeiting control of their life. But in truth, you will never be more self-determined, more in control of your destiny, than when you willingly choose to hand the reins of your life over to God. You will always know how that story ends! Those who cling desperately to managing the menial matters of life, like career and social status, think they are the captain of their destiny—

until the market crashes or the marriage fails or disease strikes. Oh, to have the courage to place your will, your plans, your security, and your future in the hands of One who always knows fully, loves perfectly, and acts justly.

It's better to be in God's hands, whatever the circumstances, than to be anywhere else. David Livingstone said that on one occasion, lions chased him up a small tree and besieged him there. He said the tree was so small that he was barely out of reach of the lions—when they'd stand on their back feet and roar and shake the little tree, he could feel the heat of their breath. "But," he said, "I had a good night and felt happier and safer in that little tree besieged by lions in the jungles of Africa in the will of God than I would have been out of the will of God in England."

The legend of the bamboo forest

The legend is told of a man who grew a bamboo forest on a mountain range. The forest loved the way the man cared for it. It felt a connection to its master—an affectionate bond that continued for years. Then one day, the master approached the forest and said, "My dear forest, we have enjoyed the beauty of this mountaintop for many years now. I come to you to ask if you are willing for me to use you for an even greater purpose than covering the mountain."

The forest, full of pride, responded, "I am willing to do whatever you need me to do."

The master said, "First, I must remove all of your branches and leaves if I am to use you for a greater purpose."

The forest considered the strange request and said, "But my beauty is in the plush foliage of my leaves and branches."

The master calmly answered, "I know. But if you are willing, I must remove them to accomplish a greater good."

Solemnly, the forest agreed.

As soon as the branches and leaves were stripped away, the master came again and said, "I imagine this will be hard for you to understand, but if I am to use you for a greater purpose, I must cut you down."

The forest pleaded, "But my very strength is in the trunks of the trees that grow to the sky. How can a greater good come from cutting me down?"

The master answered, "It is the only way. Are you willing?"

Sad, but trusting completely in the master, the forest allowed him to cut all the trees down.

"One more thing I must ask of you," the master said. "If you are to be used for a greater good, then you must allow me to split your trunks in half."

"But I will be no more!" cried the forest. "Is it not enough that I was stripped of my beauty and my strength was cut to the ground? Now you want to split my trunks in half. How can a greater good come from this?"

The master touched the trunks of one of the trees and said, "If you trust me, I will show you the greater good I have planned for you."

So, the forest allowed the master to split the trunks in half. Then the master connected the halves end to end and laid them down the mountain range into the desert, where the rain never fell. He channeled the rain that poured on the mountain down to the dry and barren wasteland, which soon became a land growing foliage and food.

Then, on the mountain range, the master went out to where his forest had been and knelt down where the trunks had been cut. Brushing away some of the debris, he saw new shoots emerging from the earth. And he smiled.

1. Ellen G. White, *Steps to Christ* (Mountain View, Calif.: Pacific Press®, 1956), 43.

2. William A. Dembski, *Intelligent Design: The Bridge Between Science & Theology* (Downers Grove, Ill.: InterVarsity Press, 1999), 25.

3. Stuart Hample and Eric Marshall, eds., *Children's Letters to God: The New Collection* (New York: Workman Publishing, 1991), 40.

4. White, *The Desire of Ages* (Nampa, Idaho: Pacific Press®, 1940), 690–693.

5. Ray Pritchard, *The Road Best Traveled: Knowing God's Will for Your Life* (Wheaton, Ill.: Crossway Books, 1995), 89.

6. Jerry Sittser, *Discovering God's Will: How to Make Every Decision With Peace and Confidence* (Grand Rapids, Mich.: Zondervan, 2000), 49.

7. Jennifer Toth, *The Mole People*, as quoted in *ChristWise Discipleship Guide—Youth*.

8. White, *Steps to Christ*, 46.

9. Chuck Swindoll, *The Mystery of God's Will* (Nashville, Tenn.: Word Publishing, 1999), 57.

Questions for Reflection

1. In what areas of your life do you struggle with the battle between what you want and what you know God wants?

2. When in your life have you prayed for God's will to be done no matter what that might mean? Reflect on why you think this prayer may be the hardest prayer to pray.

3. Of the three obstacles referred to in this chapter (freedom, control, and doubt), which troubles you most? Why?

4. In what way does knowing that Christ struggled bring comfort to you?

5. The war of the wills is more likely won through a process of surrender rather than in one pivotal moment of victory. Do you agree or disagree? Explain.

6. If God were to ask you for a deeper and more complete surrender regarding a particular aspect of your relationship with Him, what aspect would that likely be?

You Can Give God Your Will

Many are inquiring, "How am I to make the surrender of myself to God?" You desire to give yourself to Him, but you are weak in moral power, in slavery to doubt, and controlled by the habits of your life of sin. Your promises and resolutions are like ropes of sand. You cannot control your thoughts, your impulses, your affections. The knowledge of your broken promises and forfeited pledges weakens your confidence in your own sincerity, and causes you to feel that God cannot accept you; but you need not despair. What you need to understand is the true force of the will. This is the governing power in the nature of man, the power of decision, or of choice. Everything depends on the right action of the will. The power of choice God has given to men; it is theirs to exercise. You cannot change your heart, you cannot of yourself give to God its affections; but you can *choose* to serve Him. You can give Him your will; He will then work in you to will and to do according to His good pleasure. Thus your whole nature will be brought under the control of the Spirit of Christ; your affections will be centered upon Him, your thoughts will be in harmony with Him.*

*Ellen G. White, *Steps to Christ* (Mountain View, Calif.: Pacific Press®, 1956), 47.

Chapter 5

Here Comes
the Pain

An evening news program aired a special feature reporting the unorthodox methods of a last-chance reform school designed to instill discipline, responsibility, and decency in wayward teens. It showed a row of ten belligerent teens standing defiantly in the pouring rain while a drill sergeant snarled and bellowed insults in their faces. Amid the spray of spit and the barrage of commands came the recurring mantra foretelling the nature of their imminent education. The sergeant screamed, "Here comes the pain, boys. Here comes the pain!"

God is not a drill sergeant, and we are not at-risk teens (well, most of us aren't), but He did promise that sin would bring pain and death to sinners. In the aftermath of Satan's deception and Adam and Eve's disobedience, God declared, "Here comes the pain":

So the Lord God said to the serpent, "Because you have done this,

"Cursed are you above all the livestock
and all the wild animals!
You will crawl on your belly
and you will eat dust
all the days of your life.
And I will put enmity
between you and the woman,
and between your offspring and hers;

he will crush your head,
and you will strike his heel."

To the woman He said,

"I will greatly increase your pains in childbearing;
    with pain you will give birth to children.
Your desire will be for your husband,
    and he will rule over you."

To Adam he said, "Because you listened to your wife and ate from the tree about which I commanded you, 'You must not eat of it,'

"Cursed is the ground because of you;
    through painful toil you will eat of it
    all the days of your life.
It will produce thorns and thistles for you,
    and you will eat the plants of the field.
By the sweat of your brow
    you will eat your food
until you return to the ground,
    since from it you were taken;
for dust you are
    and to dust you will return."

Adam named his wife Eve, because she would become the mother of all the living.

The LORD God made garments of skin for Adam and his wife and clothed them (Genesis 3:14–21).

It is important to note that while Satan was cursed, Adam and Eve were covered. Eve did incur the pain of childbirth, and Adam would have to work hard in cultivating the soil. And solemnly, God informed both Adam and Eve that, as Paul put it, "the wages of sin is death" (Romans 6:23) and that they would surely die and return to the ground. However, part two of Paul's verse reads, "but the gift of God is eternal life." So the last sentence in the story above is crucial: "The LORD made garments of skin for Adam and his wife and *clothed them*." The promise of redemption turned Adam and Eve's despair into a long trek in which each painful step would be prompted by the hope of salvation. In a way, God warns, "Here comes the pain"—and then, in response to the suffering, He assures us, "Here am I; I'll be with you even unto the end."

This chapter enters into the conversation about how tragedy and suffering relate to God's plan for our life. It wrestles with some of the common questions that we hear or think—the ones we sometimes hesitate to say aloud. Another vein in this conversation has to do with questions and answers—not the questions we want God to answer but rather the questions God wants us to respond to. And finally, given that seeking the answer to the question *why* is an empty inquiry and finding *who* is a lifelong journey, the question *how* becomes most helpful—*how* do we negotiate tragedy and suffering? So, consider a few key questions that surface when life takes a turn for the worse.

Question #1: Does God allow bad things to happen?

A common claim often uttered in the context of tragedy is that *God didn't cause this bad thing to happen, Satan did*. I posed the following scenario to a handful of students after class: Suppose you happened upon a teenage boy mercilessly beating a five-year-old on the school playground. How would you respond? What if the school principal were standing right there as the beating was taking place but doing nothing to stop it? Whose fault would it be that the little five-year-old was being pummeled? The teenager's? How would you respond if instead of asking whose fault it was, I were to ask who was responsible for the little boy's suffering?

Clearly, in this hypothetical situation, the principal isn't directly causing the pain and the teenage boy is the agent of violence. But from our viewpoint, and especially the little boy's, the principal has the power to restrain the teenager but chooses not to. That's wrong. Surely, the principal, while he may not be directly at fault, is responsible for what is taking place. The Greek philosopher Epicurus deduced the following:

> Either God wants to abolish evil, and cannot;
> or he can, but does not want to;
> or he cannot and does not want to.
> If he wants to, but cannot, he is impotent.
> If he can, and does not want to, he is wicked.
> But, if God both can and wants to abolish evil,
> Then how come evil is in the world?[1]

While we may never openly say things like this about God, when bad things happen to people, the thought certainly troubles us. We know that God can do something about evil's random assault on people. Scripture contains records of times when God placed His hand over the mouths of the lions and protected the faithful from a fiery furnace. God is able. Pleading with Jesus to heal his son, a father said, " 'If you can do anything, take pity on us and help us' " (Mark 9:22). Jesus was astounded at the nature of the father's question. He said, " ' "If you can"? . . . Everything is possible for him who believes' " (verse 23). We can also know that God *wants* to respond to the ruin sin causes. In the case of the leper who begged Jesus, " 'If you are willing, you can make me clean,' " Jesus declared, " 'I am willing,' " and He reached out and touched him, saying, " 'Be clean.' " And the leper was restored (Mark 1:40–42). God can and has intervened, but sometimes He doesn't.

So, who is responsible? Some might slice the situation even thinner by saying that God doesn't cause bad things to happen but He does *allow* them to occur. What in the world is the difference? If God can do something about it, then the responsibility rests firmly on His shoulders. In the face of our pain, we often fail to see that God *has* done something about our suffering—He has limited its power to overcome us. Jesus said, " 'I have told you these things, so that in me you may have peace. In this world you will have trouble. But take heart! I have overcome the world' " (John 16:33).

Epicurus goes wrong when he makes God the bad guy. God is not the bad guy—He's the One to talk to about the problem of sin and the pain it causes. No one has spent more time, energy, and tears on the impact sin has made on the human experience than our Father in heaven. God, in fact, initiated the drama by saying, "Have you considered my servant Job? There is none more righteous than he." If I'd been Job, I'd have been shushing God. Who wants that kind of publicity with the enemy of souls? What did God think He was doing in telling Satan to take a closer look at Job? Certainly, Satan was behind Job's suffering—but God was behind Satan. Even though God wasn't causing Job's trouble, He was much like that principal who seemingly refrained from taking action.

Behind the grand scheme of life in this universe is a God who assumes responsibility for what takes place in His world. It doesn't help to try to excuse God for His action or apparent inaction. It doesn't help to try to subtract Him from the equation of pain and suffering—we need Him in the equation. God inserts His presence in the middle of our frustration with tragedy with this bold promise:

Who shall separate us from the love of Christ? Shall trouble or hardship or persecution or famine or nakedness or danger or sword? As it is written:

"For your sake we face death all day long;

we are considered as sheep to be slaughtered."

No, in all these things we are more than conquerors through him who loved us. For I am convinced that neither death nor life, neither angels nor demons, neither the present nor the future, nor any powers, neither height nor depth, nor anything else in all creation, will be able to separate us from the love of God that is in Christ Jesus our Lord (Romans 8:35–39).

Question #2: Why ask why?

When trouble hits people unexpectedly, the *why* question often arises. Amid the perpetual beeps and swooshes of life-support equipment in the ICU, a tear-worn grandmother exclaims, "God's going to have a lot of explaining to do about this one, that's for sure." I often wonder if we insist on answers about the *why* of tragedy because the random punches of suffering pound us in a way that seems unusually unjust. It's possible that when tragedy strikes, we want someone to take responsibility for the pain. It's one thing to suffer, but it is unbearable to feel that no one has the authority to make it right or the power to make the pain go away. We know that the Bible says the wages of sin is death, so we might be able to consider suffering logically when it happens to someone else. But when we become that someone else, we tighten our fists in anger. We might know bad things happen in a sinful world, but we don't want those things to happen to us.

Some people think Romans 8:28 is the magic verse that settles all of life's disappointments by saying everything that happens will turn out for good or is God's will. Stop right there! More people have shaken their heads at funerals, hospital beds, cancer wards, gravesides, and war zones after hearing people prop God up with the insensitive nonanswers, "It must have been God's will" or "Everything that happens does so for our own good."

Trying to explain why bad things happen is probably futile and unproductive. The experience leaves us empty and confused. We simply won't comprehend the nature of all these events this side of heaven. All our logic and our coherent explanations get blown away in the midst of our pain. In his attempt to be honest about tragedy, Chris Tiegreen says that the fact that we suffer shouldn't surprise us: "If you've lived any time at all in this world, you've experienced pain. You've seen people suffer, and you've seen people die. You've been offended, and you've been guilty of offenses. You've cried yourself to sleep, and you've made others cry. Though you strive to escape the threat of evil, you know that as long as you dwell on this broken planet, you never will."[2]

For centuries, believers have clung to God faithfully despite never getting a satisfying explanation for their pain. We can discover a way to live God's will for our life when we consider the character of this God who sometimes acts and sometimes doesn't. We can survive the trip through the valley of the shadow of death if He goes with us, showing us how to heal, how to overcome.

Question #3: Is tragedy some form of cosmic punishment?

When the going gets tough, the tough often wonder what they did wrong. We typically assume that if trouble comes, we must have angered God by misbehavior or missed behavior. This line of thinking isn't theologically sound nor is it logical, but the undercurrent of guilt pulls at our foundations the way the receding tide compels us to come along. Maybe the source of this kind of thinking lies in the way people perceived the pagan gods in ancient times. Certainly, during the time of Christ, people held the notion that God uses tragedy to give people what they deserve. When the disciples noticed a man who had been blind from birth, they inquired of Jesus, " 'Rabbi, who sinned, this man or his parents, that he was born blind?' " (John 9:2).

That was such a ridiculous question! What would have prompted God to punish the poor kid with blindness at birth, before he even had the chance to do something bad? Or did God look into the crystal ball of this young man's life and see a future filled with self-absorbed debauchery and so zapped him with blindness at birth? There is just no end to the problematic line of thinking stirred up by such a notion.

What about the parents? Doesn't the Bible say that the sins of one generation pass on to the next? Yes, but the Scriptures also say that Abraham's father was an idolater, yet Abraham became the father of the children of God. The question remains: Are tragedies the result of our misbehavior or the opportunities we've missed? I must confess that when things go wrong, I tend to wonder, *God, are You trying to tell me something?*

Paul explained that "sin entered the world through one man, and death through sin, and in this way death came to all men" (Romans 5:12). However, when he warned us that "the wages of sin is death," he also reminded us that "the gift of God is eternal life" (6:23). While God " 'causes his sun to rise on the evil and the good,' " He also " 'sends rain on the righteous and the unrighteous' " (Matthew 5:45). And even though Jesus assured us that adversity would be a part of our journey, He also offered His people peace, saying, " 'Take heart! I have overcome the world' " (John 16:33). Further, we are promised that "what God has prepared for those who love him" exceeds everything that human beings have ever seen, heard, or even imagined (1 Corinthians 2:9). So, even "though you have not seen him, you love him; and even though you do not see him now, you believe in him and are filled with an inexpressible and glorious joy, for you are receiving the goal of your faith, the salvation of your souls" (1 Peter 1:8, 9).

What these promises tell us is true. For centuries, many have endured indescribable grief by hanging on the hope that God's Word is sure. By faith, believers have clawed and clambered their way through the darkness of trauma and disappointment, finding new places to see. Consider how Asaph, the writer of some of the psalms, found a way to see.

Asaph's journey

Truly God is good to the upright,
    to those who are pure in heart (Psalm 73:1, NRSV).

What a great opening statement! It is very Israel-like. It conveys the right information. It is exactly what people are supposed to say about God. It is "the Truth."

At one camp meeting I attended, a speaker stood up and wailed, "God is good!" and the congregation roared back without needing a cue, "All the time!" The speaker was pleased with the response and screamed, "All the time!" and the congregation roared, "God is good!" As the chanting continued, "God is good—all the time. All the time—God is good," a woman in front of me rose to her feet, murmuring, "Not to me. Not today."

The puzzle wasn't hard to put together: "God may be good—but not to me. God may be good all the time, but not today." I watched that woman walk out, unable to listen to the chanting throng. Perhaps she could have empathized with Asaph.

No sooner did Asaph's cliché fall from his lips than the "but" emerged to wrinkle the nice, neat religion. "But" signifies a dramatic shift in the direction of thought, ideas, or action.

> But as for me, my feet had almost stumbled;
>   my steps had almost slipped (verse 2, NRSV).

Why? What happened that almost caused Asaph to stumble and fall in his faith in God? Even with all the right words and correct theology, something so shook his world that he was ready to toss his faith in God aside.

> For I was envious of the arrogant;
>   I saw the prosperity of the wicked.
>
> For they have no pain;
>   their bodies are sound and sleek.
> They are not in trouble as others are;
>   they are not plagued like other people.
> Therefore pride is their necklace;
>   violence covers them like a garment.
> Their eyes swell out with fatness;
>   their hearts overflow with follies.
> They scoff and speak with malice;
>   loftily they threaten oppression.
> They set their mouths against heaven,
>   and their tongues range over the earth.
>
> Therefore the people turn and praise them,
>   and find no fault in them.
> And they say, "How can God know?
>   Is there knowledge in the Most High?"
> Such are the wicked;
>   always at ease, they increase in riches (verses 3–12, NRSV).

Asaph looked at the reality around him and observed that his formula had broken down. God is supposed to look after His people; but it appeared from where he was standing that God is not "good to the upright." In fact, Asaph witnessed the very opposite of what his theology stated to be true: The wicked flourish. Not only do they flourish, but they also flaunt their prosperity in the face of God, saying, "How can God know? Is there knowledge in the Most High?" Asaph's faith was challenged because his experience contradicted the information in his head. What he saw and felt and heard was in direct contradistinction to what he had been taught about God.

Has crisis ever sideswiped the core beliefs you hold? It remains true today that tragedy, injustice, and pain hammer even the people who faithfully serve God. And all the religious mantras and Christian clichés in the world cannot match the sheer force of the storm of life. Knowledge has never been enough. Consider how the truth that gets catalogued in our minds is so easily canned when life knocks us down.

> All in vain I have kept my heart clean
>> and washed my hands in innocence.
> For all day long I have been plagued,
>> and am punished every morning (verses 13, 14, NRSV).

Maybe an illness plagued Asaph. Perhaps the faithful priest suffered from an affliction that hampered his ministry. Essentially, he was complaining, "I thought God was supposed to be good to the upright! Not to me. Not today. It simply doesn't make sense. Reality seems to contradict God's claims, so why not throw in the towel?" But Asaph didn't give up on God. Instead, he described a timely turning point in his despair.

> If I had said, "I will talk on in this way,"
>> I would have been untrue to the circle of your children.
> But when I thought how to understand this,
>> it seemed to me a wearisome task (verses 15, 16, NRSV).

In other words, Asaph was saying, "If I continued to keep thinking and talking to myself this way, I would surely have forsaken God." He recognized that while his theology was inadequate, his experience and perceptions weren't entirely trustworthy either. He concluded that he didn't rightly understand what was going on. He knew cognitively and also by his lived experience that God is good and His promises are true. But what he saw didn't align with what should be: The wicked are blessed! They prosper and poke fun at God, and God is silent while the righteous are sick and broken! Neither Asaph's knowledge nor his experience—nor the two of them combined—enabled him to make sense of what he was seeing.

There comes a point when knowledge and experience alone are not sufficient to carry us through crisis. Asaph was in a teachable moment, and what he would choose to do in response was critical. The same is true for every believer. What is our response when our knowledge contradicts our experience—when the rules we live by and the beliefs we affirm are impotent against the trauma that we continually hear, feel, and see?

Some might be tempted to deny that their experience is real, covering it up with texts and trite sayings. They shore up their smile with Bible promises and swallow the frustration in the name of faith. They deny the truth of their experience, saying, "This too shall pass" or "It's not as bad as it seems" or "God's timing is not our timing." Dress it up any way you like, but it is still denial. The same is true for those who jump ship and dump their beliefs overboard when life gets unbearable. We're tempted to deny what we know because what we see around us speaks with greater volume. But notice what Asaph did when his teachable moment came.

> But when I thought how to understand this,
>   it seemed to me a wearisome task,
> until I went into the sanctuary of God;
>   then I perceived their end (verses 16, 17, NRSV).

Asaph didn't turn to his knowledge or his experience. He didn't rub his eyes and reexamine life to determine whether he was seeing the world clearly. This faith-shaken priest could have cracked open a book on theology or perhaps listened to a popular self-help tape series that might have inspired him to be positive and proactive. But instead, he turned his feet to the place where God promised to dwell with His people—the sanctuary. Asaph made his way into the very presence of God—for comfort, maybe, but mostly for clarity. The sanctuary is rich with meaning, symbolism, and the means for dealing with the problem of sin.

In the sanctuary of God, Asaph began to understand what was happening in the world around him. Did he discover some new angle of truth in the lampstand or a word-picture of God's grace in the sacrifice? No. It was when Asaph *entered the presence of God* that his mind and heart were transformed.

> Truly you set them in slippery places;
>   you make them fall to ruin.
> How they are destroyed in a moment,
>   swept away utterly by terrors!
> They are like a dream when one awakes;
>   on awaking you despise their phantoms (verses 18–20, NRSV).

What changed Asaph's song from despair to confidence in God's ways? Everything changed when the priest chose to view the events of life from the reference point of the plan of salvation in the very presence of God (the sanctuary). The psalm doesn't reveal what happened between God and Asaph, and maybe that's the point—the renewed vision cannot be described, only experienced.

Another beautiful truth that emerges from Asaph's testimony reaches beyond what he learned about God and people to what he discovered about himself:

> When my soul was embittered,
>> when I was pricked in heart,
> I was stupid and ignorant;
>> I was like a brute beast toward you (verses 21, 22, NRSV).

Standing in God's presence and looking fully at His plan of salvation exposes who we really are—sinners. Shortsighted. Heavy-minded. Imbalanced. We launch our words about God, life, and justice with very little knowledge and very little sense of the presence of God. But standing next to God we see differently; we see better. Listen to Asaph's testimony as he steps out of the sanctuary. Listen to his refined knowledge powered by a personal experience with God. Listen to his new song!

> Nevertheless I am continually with you;
>> *you hold my right hand.*
> You guide me with your counsel,
>> and afterward you will receive me with honor.
> Whom have I in heaven but you?
>> And there is nothing on earth that I desire other than you.
> My flesh and my heart may fail,
>> but God is the strength of my heart and my portion forever.
>
> Indeed, *those who are far from you* will perish;
>> you put an end to those who are false to you.
> But for me *it is good to be near God*;
>> I have made the Lord GOD my refuge,
>>> to tell of all your works (verses 23–28, NRSV; emphasis added).

Asaph discovered that we can try to hang on to God through our beliefs. We can attempt to fasten ourselves to Him by our theology. We can reach out for Him with good deeds, and we can grasp at spiritual epiphanies. But when tragedy strikes, all these good things won't save us. However, though our grip on God is feeble, His grip on us is sure. Asaph declared, "You hold my right hand." Oh what a reality check it must have been for Asaph to learn that when nothing else will hold us up, God's abiding grace will never let us go.

Asaph revealed the "difference-maker" in his renewed walk with God: He learned that those who are far from God will perish, and it was good for him to be near God. The presence of the Lord made all the difference. And the God who is Emmanuel will make the difference for us in our darkest moments.

We often assume that if God isn't good to us even in our trauma, then He obviously isn't good at all. *God is good, and He is sovereign. When God doesn't seem to be either good or sovereign, we can safely assume there's something wrong with our vision.* God's action or inaction may never make any sense as long as we stand at a distance. Where we stand makes all the difference in the way we perceive the world around us. God's action or inaction will never make sense when we are far from His presence. But if we will choose to dwell with God in heartache, we'll see things in a new way. That new perspective may eventually give us something to sing about.

God's questions, our answers

It's only natural to have questions for God. When you don't have all the information, ask questions. But I believe something matters more to God than answering the questions we have for Him. Consider for a moment the questions He asks us. What answers does God seek from us? Maybe the secret to a deeper walk with God lies in our response to the questions He asks. Scripture contains hundreds of such questions. God's questions challenge the mind and expose the will.

In Scripture, the questions God asks initiate watershed events. Adam and Eve. Moses. Elijah. The disciples. Mary. Examine the scenarios in which God asks a question, and discover the continental divide between life and death, hope and despair, growth and failure—a watershed response from one side of life to the other. The questions God asks are huge, life changing, mind-altering.

There's another interesting facet about the power of God's questions. In every scenario in Scripture, the questions God asks people reveal what is important to Him. In a way, God's queries give us a glimpse of His character. You can learn a lot about people simply by examining the types of questions they ask. The questions God asks are windows to His heart and doorways to His plan for our life. Consider a few questions that God popped, and see if you can discover something about Him as well as something about yourself:

"Where are you?" God wants to know if we know how far away we are.

"Where are your accusers?" God wants us to answer aloud so we can hear from our own lips the timeless truth of grace.

"Who do you think I am?" The future of the Christian movement leans fully on the answer we give.

"Why are you so afraid?" Jesus invites us to name one thing that is bigger than His promise and provision for our future.

"Why are you laughing?" God wants to know what's funny about His plan for our life.

"Who are you looking for?" Jesus reminds us to be deliberate about the focus of our lives.

"Do you know what I have done to you?" God quizzes us on His chief lesson on service.

"What is in your hand?" God wonders if we have room in our life for Him to do extraordinary things with the ordinary routine of our day.

However, we find in John 11 the question that captures perfectly the burning desire Christ has for people drowning in grief. Jesus' friend Lazarus has died. When Martha, a sister of Lazarus, comes out to meet Jesus, she spills her heart out before Him, saying, " 'Lord, . . . if you had been here, my brother would not have died' " (verse 21). Jesus then reminds her of the hope of the resurrection. Martha "knows" about the resurrection. Still, sadness overwhelms her. Jesus could have let it pass, but He reminds her who He is and then asks a question of Martha: "Jesus said to her, 'I am the resurrection and the life. He who believes in me will live, even though he dies; and whoever lives and believes in me will never die. *Do you believe this?*' " (verses 25, 26; emphasis added).

I can imagine the Savior taking Martha's face in His hands and looking straight into her eyes. I can see Him peering into her soul, longing to give her the only thing that will help to heal her broken heart. Jesus asks a question that we all might thoughtlessly answer with a Yes. But Jesus knows that hope will spring in Martha's heart the moment she speaks the words, "Yes, I believe." I wonder if this might be the most important question God has ever asked. Above all other questions, God must long to have His children answer this particular one in our darkest moments: " 'Do you believe this?' " (verse 26).

Do you believe that God is telling the truth when He claims that death is only a sleep?

Do you believe Him when He tells you that He is preparing a place for you to live with Him in eternity?

Do you believe that His arms hold you in your anguish?

Do you believe that even if you say goodbye to people you love, you will see them again?

Do you believe that God will come back and make things new again?

Do you believe that there will be no more pain, no more sorrow, no more suffering, no more death, no more crying when He makes the earth new again?

Do you believe this?

Ask your questions of God or keep them close to your heart—that's your choice. But whichever you choose, answer His question for you, because in the questions God asks we find a window into His heart and discover a doorway to His will for our life.

How to hang on

I was trying to explain to high school students that while hanging on to God during seasons of pain or loss isn't easy, it is the only thing to do. Nathan observed my struggle and volunteered an amazing metaphor for the class to consider. He asked if we'd ever seen a climbing wall. The face of the wall, he said, is covered with bumps and knobs of various sizes and shapes that people use to climb the wall. Some of these protrusions are as big as a brick, providing an easy-to-use hand- or foothold. Others are tiny, only a nub—but you can rest the full force of your weight on that little nub.

Sometimes in life we have broad places on which to put our feet. At other times, we have only a little nub—perhaps just one Bible verse or the example of one fellow believer. But like a nub on the climbing wall, even though it's not much, it is enough—enough to hold our full weight.

About a month after Nathan gave us this illustration, he died in an automobile accident. Then we were forced to practice the principle of faith he had so appropriately conveyed to us.

While the Bible contains many stories of miracles and supernatural interventions, the pages of my own experience are blank. In the last ten years, I have stood at the side of many hospital beds, praying for a miracle. From the bedside to the graveside, I've been haunted by the times when God's will didn't include a healing or a miracle. And I know I'm not alone.

At first I concluded that there must be something wrong with me. Then I thought there must be something wrong with God. But when I look across the pews at church, I see moms and dads who have buried their children and who are still coming into God's presence and listening, praying, and singing. They're hanging on by a nub, but they're still singing. I witness believers extend forgiveness to people who have taken their children's life in senseless acts of violence. You can see it in their faces—they're standing on a nub, but they are standing. And I wonder which is the greater miracle—the gift of healing from cancer or the gift of living joyfully in the sure hope of a new day? Which is more otherworldly?

It is truly amazing when a doctor saves a life or a firefighter rescues a child from a burning building. But how much more supernatural is the believer's banking of every tear, every ounce of pain, on a promise made by Someone they've never seen? Truly, the miraculous is all around us in the form of faithful believers who continue to stay with God no matter what comes their way. Perhaps some of the insights they've shared might be helpful to you or someone you know.

Community. The only way to navigate the troublous seas of tragedy is alongside others. Solomon observed,

> Two are better than one,
>> because they have a good return for their work:
> If one falls down,
>> his friend can help him up.
> But pity the man who falls
>> and has no one to help him up! (Ecclesiastes 4:9, 10).

In *The Samson Syndrome*, Mark Atteberry examined the life of the man who could have been one of the greatest heroes in the Bible. Atteberry said, "What's striking is that Samson, by choice, traveled alone. We never see him with a sidekick, a buddy, or a mentor. Unlike Moses, who had Aaron; or Joshua, who had Caleb; or David, who had Jonathan; or Paul, who had Barnabas and Silas, . . . Samson had nobody. He wandered the roads of life all by himself and paid a terrible price."[3] Like

Samson, too many people try to travel the road of loss and disappointment alone.

The story is told of a little boy who noticed that the old man who lived next door was sitting on his front porch and weeping. He had just returned from a funeral. Instinctively, the young boy made his way over to help. Without hesitation, he climbed onto the lap of the sobbing old man and sat quietly.

The boy's mother watched the whole scene. When it was time for bed, she asked her sweet little son what he'd said to their neighbor. The little boy replied, "I didn't say anything. I just helped him cry."

The apostle Paul urged believers to "rejoice with those who rejoice; [and] mourn with those who mourn" (Romans 12:15). The true meaning of community becomes clear when believers walk the shadowy road together. Most often, very little needs to be said.

Search. When your world falls apart, search for the who and not for the why. There are many things we don't know about God, but we do know that He wants to be known. Jesus prayed, " 'This is eternal life: that they may know you, the only true God, and Jesus Christ, whom you have sent' " (John 17:3). We find the peace that passes understanding in the warmth of God's presence. James pled with believers to "come near to God and he will come near to you" (James 4:8). People whom trouble has struck have the choice of flinging away their faith in God or clinging to what still remains.

Arthur John Gossip was an eccentric, opinionated preacher in Aberdeen, Scotland, in the early twentieth century. When his wife died, leaving him alone, he titled the next sermon he preached "When Life Tumbles In, Then What?" Ray Pritchard quotes a few of his words: "I do not understand this life of ours. But still less can I comprehend how people in trouble and loss and bereavement can fling away peevishly from the Christian faith. In God's name, fling to what? Have we not lost enough without losing that too?"[4]

Surely, God can hold us even while we question what we see and feel. In fact, as believers search for God in those moments, they will know God in ways many will only wonder about.

Share. As you make your way through pain, you will discover that you are refreshed and encouraged by others who know pain in a similar way. Then you'll be supremely qualified to hold the hand of someone else walking in darkness. Although you may want to run every time you're near someone who is suffering, draw close to that person. They'll find strength in the fact that you understand. The community that meant so much to you needs you to help someone else.

Consider the following passage from God's Word, as it conveys the need for you to share yourself and perhaps your story with someone who is hurting: "Praise be to the God and Father of our Lord Jesus Christ, the Father of compassion and the God of all comfort, who comforts us in all our troubles, so that we can comfort those in any trouble with the comfort we ourselves have received from God. For just as the sufferings of Christ flow over into our lives, so also through Christ our comfort overflows" (2 Corinthians 1:3–5).

When I was in Africa with a large group of students, Kris, a college student who had lost his little brother in a house fire, shared his journey with hundreds of Zambians gathered at night under a large mango tree. I watched the hearts of those listening resonate with his story, for they knew pain and understood loss. Kris's voice became stronger and more passionate with every word he spoke, as he testified to God's power and His plan for a home with no more tears, no more sorrow, no more crying, no more death. Perhaps we find reprieve from our pain in helping others with theirs. I have watched the heroes of faith enough now to know that although they hurt, they hate sin with a passion and hope for heaven with immeasurable strength.

Jerry Sittser summarized his journey through tragedy this way:

> I remind myself that suffering is not unique to us. It is the destiny of humanity. If this world were the only one there is, the suffering has the final say and we are a sorry lot. But generations of faithful Christians have gone before and will come after, and they believed or will believe what I believe in the depths of my soul. Jesus is at the center of it all. He defeated sin and death through his crucifixion and resurrection. Then light gradually dawns once again in my heart, and hope returns. I find reason and courage to keep going and to continue believing. Once again my soul increases its capacity for hope as well as for sadness. I end up believing with greater depth and joy than I had before, even in my sorrow.[5]

Discovering God's will isn't a journey around adversity but a choice to allow God to carry you through it. I believe God's promises are sure even when our circumstances seem unbearable. I love the story about the little boy who was carrying a basket full of groceries while shopping with his father.

The basket became quite full, and a clerk noticed that the little boy was struggling to manage the weight as he bravely lumbered toward the checkout line. The clerk asked, "Do you need help with that basket, young man?" to which the boy replied, "No. My father knows how much I can carry."

---

1. Epicurus, quoted in Lee Strobel, *The Case for Faith: A Journalist Investigates the Toughest Objections to Christianity* (Grand Rapids, Mich.: Zondervan, 2000), 25.

2. Chris Tiegreen, *Why a Suffering World Makes Sense* (Grand Rapids, Mich.: Baker Books, 2006), 20.

3. As cited in Mark Atteberry's book *Walking With God on the Road You Never Wanted to Travel* (Nashville, Tenn.: Thomas Nelson, 2005), 38.

4. Ray Pritchard, *Keep Believing* (Chicago, Ill.: Moody Press, 1997), 18.

5. Jerry Sittser, *A Grace Disguised* (Grand Rapids, Mich.: Zondervan, 1995), 152.

Questions for Reflection

1. What trying seasons have you endured that have caused you to question the nature of God's will as it relates to suffering? How have you managed to negotiate those difficult times?

2. Reflect on the times when you've heard people offer trite, empty explanations for the painful experiences people face. How do you react in such a scenario?

3. God may not cause tragedy, but He assumes responsibility for making it right. Do you agree or disagree? Explain your response.

4. Why do you think asking *why* is such a common response to tragedy? To what degree does an explanation help someone who is experiencing trauma?

5. In what way do you resonate with Asaph's song? In what ways were his experience and his testimony helpful to you?

6. Which of God's questions do you think need to be answered? Which one do you think begs a response from you today?

Part III

Doing God's Will

Chapter 6

Calling, Careers, and Other Conundrums

"I think I'll be a preacher when I grow up," a young boy confided to his mother.

"That's a wonderful calling," the mother said, "but why do you want to be a preacher?"

"Well," the youngster replied, "I figure I'll have to go to church all my life anyway, and it's harder to sit than to stand up and holler."[1]

It might be interesting to survey the clergy to see how many men and women of the cloth were inclined toward ministry for the same reason!

It's not just seven-year-olds who ruminate on their choice of vocation. High school seniors bounce all over the map, touting prophecies about their career path. Some will immediately enter a trade and find work. Others will go to college, where they're supposed to choose a major course of study. Some college students don't succumb to the hurry. They find a way to cram four years of college into six years.

College students often experience a tremendous amount of stress if they feel uncertain about a major. One described the pressure this way: "I feel like I'm on a fast-moving conveyor belt headed toward somewhere—maybe it's a giant buzz-saw, like in James Bond movies. The sense that I need to do something now to save myself from failure is real, very real."

I think we're all searching for something more than a good job; we're searching for our calling. Time is precious, and we consume too much of our lives in making ends meet. For this reason, young and old take their searching seriously.

My research on student missionaries (college students who spend a year abroad in service) showed that many students chose to take a year from school to serve abroad primarily because of their indecision about a career or confusion about a sense of calling:

"I didn't have any real direction in college," reported one student, while another revealed how troubling it was to be uncertain, saying, "I didn't know what my major was and I was kind of scared about that." Students noted that their lack of direction did not emerge from a lack of trying. Some studied nursing, then interior design, [and] finally in frustration one reported, "I hated everything and I just told my mom, 'I'm leaving, bye.'" Out of this urgency to discover their place in a professional track, students clearly hoped the experience of serving would provide "a nice time to figure everything out." Another student reported that they chose to serve for a year "just to get some perspective and find out really if that is what I wanted to do." Other students hoped to possibly "get some focus" or simply "realign" their focus.

While some might have reported that they had "no clue" what they wanted to do, others had notions about a specific career that they wanted to test. "I was thinking about doing teaching but I wasn't sure so I wanted to try that out," claimed a student. The "trial by fire" approach to sifting out their career conundrums became a theme throughout their reporting. One student admitted, "I was pre-med at one point and I was struggling. I wasn't sure." Another medical student said, "I wanted to know whether this [pre-med] was actually what I wanted to do." Some considered the SM experience as a way to "test" and "see" if they could handle the career choice they had already made. The desire for clarity caused many to stop the "traditional" educational process because a year of service was reputed to authenticate or expose any career uncertainties.[2]

But college students don't own exclusive claim to suffering stress because of having to make decisions about their careers. Throughout the adult years, either internal impetuses or external opportunities prompt many to shift professions. A business executive will take his experience to the classroom. A doctor will devote herself to politics. Engineers will become missionaries, and writers become ranchers.

Even referring to what we "become" is dubious. It is as though our whole makeup, our sense of "who we are," changes when we change jobs. Students also experience this. One day they graduate from college, and the next day they start at an accounting firm—they go from being a student to being an accountant in just twenty-four hours. But perhaps we need to see our identity in a more enduring way. Part of learning to live God's will for our life includes knowing the difference between vocation and career. The word *vocation* comes from the Latin word *vocare*, which means "to call or summon." We speak of becoming aware of a vocation as "sensing a calling" or "hearing a voice." A career is merely a job category.

Compare two responses of students questioned about their reason for choosing to go into nursing. One professed, "I'm going into nursing because the hours are flexible, I can travel, and it pays pretty well," while another replied, "I'm going into nursing because I want to help people who are sick or in pain, I can pay attention to details, and it fits my lifestyle." To me, the first statement seems to be focused on the most expedient way to accommodate life with work. The latter statement conveys a sense of calling and a desire to integrate life and work.

Something that makes a difference

I believe most people want to work in a way that resonates with who they are. One of the marks of adulthood is a thirst for doing something that makes a difference as well as something that makes sense. In the book *Made to Count*, authors Bob Reccord and Randy Singer focus on what causes people to demand so much of their vocation. The research they reference conveys the worry people feel that their work doesn't really matter. They report, "By far the most voiced response strikes deep at the heart of all of us: to come to life's end without having made a significant difference. Atychiphobia. The fear of failure."[3]

Po Bronson echoes this urge to know what we should do with our lives, testifying, "We want to know where we are headed—not to spoil our own ending by ruining the surprise, but we want to ensure that when the ending comes, it won't be shallow. We will have done something. We will not have squandered our time here."[4]

Po Bronson wrote for TV shows and magazine columns until his opportunities diminished into unemployment and he found himself looking for work with his first child on the way. As a talented writer, Bronson could have easily managed to find "work," but his questions about what he *should* do urged him to spend a year embedded in the lives of people who were going through a similar personal metamorphosis. His research uncovered stories of everyday people in search of meaning and guidance. Bronson explained, "Looking for guidance and courage at this crossroads, I became intrigued by people who had unearthed their true calling, or at least those who were willing to try. Those who fought with the seduction of money, intensity, and novelty, but overcame their allure. Those who broke away from the chorus to learn the sound of their own voice. Nothing seemed braver to me than facing up to one's own identity, and filtering out the chatter that tells us to be someone we're not."[5]

At the center of our search for God's plan lies a curiosity about who we are. God knew who we were before we were born; David wrote, "Your eyes saw my unformed body" (Psalm 139:16). Paul also conveyed the fact that God knows us, claiming that God "chose us in him before the creation of the world" (Ephesians 1:4). Again, God comes right out with His own beautiful mission statement. " 'I know the plans I have for you,' declares the LORD, 'plans to prosper you and not to harm you, plans to give you hope and a future' " (Jeremiah 29:11). If you ever wonder about whether you are in God's plan or out of it, refresh your mind with Paul's promise to fellow travelers, "He who began a good work in you will carry it on to completion until the day of Christ Jesus" (Philippians 1:6). As believers in Christ, our sense of who we are is shaped by more than just what's inside our hearts.

It may be that when some people sense a calling, they are hearing a couple of different voices. First, they are listening to the way they are wired. We emerge from childhood with inherent qualities and acquired interests. Our life experiences shape us in a way that makes us passionate about some things and indifferent to others. These passions can be wholesome or unhealthy, but they are a real part of each of us. Second, we look to God either to bless our interests or to awaken in us a vision of something that might be even more interesting to us—something that we aren't aware of. So we pray, "Dear God, show me what I should do!"

Remember, to a certain degree, this prayer has already been answered in God's Word: You should receive Christ as your Savior. You should live as a child of God. You should strive to become like Christ. You should be grateful, kind, filled with the Holy Spirit. The key is to avoid separating the biggest things we do from the smaller things we do. In fact, the goal is to integrate them. It is a matter of integrated priorities.

At weddings, graduations, and other events, I have often used a timeless object lesson that calls for organizing our life according to our priorities. I start with a glass jar, a bowl of raw rice, and a pile of rocks. I tell the audience, "This jar represents our daily life; the rocks represent our core values, beliefs, and eternal commitments; and the rice represents all the little things of life."

I pour rice into the jar until it's half full. Then I say, "Simply taking life as it comes is like pouring the rice into the jar—little things may fill up half our lives. But every once in a while, we sense conviction that we need something more substantial to live by, so we try to fit the rocks—our core beliefs and values—in with the rice."

I try to put the rocks into the jar, but because it's half full of rice, I can fit only a few in. I explain, "We may be able to fit a couple in, but inevitably, some will be left out. Some people live this way, not sure of how to integrate the most important things into their busy lives."

Next, I dump the jar out, put all the rocks in it, and then slowly pour the rice in, filling the cracks and crevices between the rocks. And I say, "Perhaps the better way is to begin with the rocks, making sure all of them fit in. Then, as we live our daily grind, the things of life fit into place. This is what I call a 'well-ordered life.' "

A well-ordered life

David prayed to God, "Order my steps in thy word: and let not any iniquity have dominion over me" (Psalm 119:133, KJV). Charles Spurgeon preached a helpful sermon, "The Well-Ordered Life," on this passage. Here is a brief excerpt from this masterpiece:

> "Order," says David, or as some read, "direct," "set straight," "appoint," "firmly establish," or, "rightly frame my steps." David, looking abroad upon nature, saw order ruling everywhere in Heaven above and on the earth beneath and even among the fowl of the air and the fish of the sea. He desired, therefore, to fall into rank and keep the harmony of the universe. He was not afraid of being laughed at for living by method and rule, for he saw method and rule to be Divine institutions. He did not aspire to a random life, or envy the free-livers, whose motto is, "Do whatever you like."
>
> He had no lusts to be his own master—he wished in all things to be governed by the superior and all-perfect will of God. In the

text, King David bows in homage to the King of kings—he enlists in the army of the Lord of Hosts and asks for marching orders and Grace to obey them. Note the next word[s], "My steps." He is anxious as to details. David does not say, "Order the whole of my pilgrimage." He may mean that, but his expression is more expressive and painstaking—he would have each single step ordered in holiness—he would enjoy heavenly guidance in each minute portion of his journey towards Heaven.[6]

Charles Spurgeon noticed in David's prayer an earnest desire for God's guidance in every aspect of his life. Like David, many long to have God order their footsteps in such a way that their life makes sense and makes a difference. Whatever stage in life we find ourselves in, there are a few questions to consider as we negotiate through the decisions we make about our vocation.

Question #1: What are my beliefs?

Make a list of the kind of jobs you feel fit your personal ethics and moral framework. Some professions may run contrary to your beliefs. The Bible is filled with examples of people who refused to compromise the core convictions of their heart. Joseph had every earthly reason to fudge on his personal purity for the sake of his career. Potiphar's wife made overt sexual advances toward him, but the Bible says, "He refused. 'With me in charge,' he told her, 'my master does not concern himself with anything in the house; everything he owns he has entrusted to my care. No one is greater in this house than I am. My master has withheld nothing from me except you, because you are his wife. How then could I do such a wicked thing and sin against God?' And though she spoke to Joseph day after day, he refused to go to bed with her or even be with her" (Genesis 39:8–10).

How easy it would have been for Joseph to rationalize his whole scenario as a sort of hiccup in God's rule. He might have murmured in his heart the question, "How could this possibly be God's plan for my life?" He might have become discouraged, wondering why God would let his brothers mistreat him with violence—attempt to murder him. However, in spite of the circumstances and the temptations Potiphar's wife presented, Joseph kept his beliefs firmly before him. Not just once but daily, Joseph resisted and ran from the seductions of another man's wife. What is so powerful about Joseph's story is that his faithfulness to God fostered tremendous success—well beyond anything Potiphar or his wife could have offered. No, Joseph heard the call to leadership, and the voice in his heart demanded unwavering devotion to God and the ethics of heaven.

Examine the story in Daniel 1 of the three Hebrew boys whose only glimmer of hope seemed to reside in playing the king's game of mental and religious reorientation. Instead of going along with the officially prescribed diet, the boys refused to compromise their convictions even if it meant death. The issue wasn't entirely about food; it was about devotion to God and an opportunity to make His ways known.

Given enough time, the human heart can rationalize any behavior, any business transaction, any unethical endeavor. So, before you look at the many opportunities that are before you as a vocation, take a long look at your beliefs. What are your nonnegotiable values; what are you unwilling to compromise? Make a list.

Question #2: What are my character qualities?

The apostle Paul honored Priscilla and Aquila, claiming, "they risked their lives for me" (Romans 16:4). Epenetus was a groundbreaking pioneer. Paul said he was "the first convert to Christ in the province of Asia" (verse 5). Mary was reputed to be a hard worker (verse 6). Andronicus and Junias, relatives of Paul who were imprisoned with him, were bedrock believers in Christ before Paul was (verse 7). Ampliatus was loveable (verse 8). Urbanus was Paul's fellow worker (verse 9). Tryphena and Tryphosa, as well as Persis, were known for being hard workers for the Lord (verse 12). Gaius was known for his hospitality (verse 23). Throughout this last chapter of the book of Romans, Paul named names of people most of us know nothing about. Not only did he name them, but he also described the qualities these people were known for. What are you known for? What character qualities are evident in your life?

Set aside the temptation to downplay your qualities, and examine your history. Invite others to share what they think are your greatest strengths. It might seem awkward at first, but the people who love you and know you know that your intent is to find your calling.

Craig, one of my students, asked me this question, and I shocked him with my answer: "Craig, as long as I have known you, I have observed how calm you are. On our mission trip, when the generator failed, everyone went crazy. But you quietly settled people down and refilled the machine with fuel. When a fight broke out in the dorm, you calmly separated the feuding parties without losing control, even when you received a blow to the nose. Craig, you are as cool as the other side of a pillow. You are self-controlled and thoughtful when things get out of control." Craig had never once considered that attribute of his character as a clue to what his calling might be.

Several months later, Craig became an emergency medical technician. Eventually, he enrolled in a nursing program while working as a volunteer emergency responder. He now is a lead nurse for a busy E.R. unit. Craig claims, "Sometimes you have to listen to the people you trust to get an idea about what you are good at. In my case, I never thought of self-control as a trait that might influence my calling."

Marcus Buckingham and Donald Clifton suggest that "spontaneous reactions, yearnings, rapid learning, and satisfaction" reveal clues to discovering your vocation.[7] Your initial reaction to stressful situations or problems may give you a clue as to some of your strengths. If a co-worker calls in sick, straining the rest of the staff, and your response is, "I wonder if someone is going to bring them chicken soup?" then perhaps one of your qualities is compassion.

Often, our yearnings emerge in childhood. Mozart's did. He had composed his first symphony by the time he was twelve. The Bible says, "Delight yourself in the LORD and he will give you the desires of your heart" (Psalm 37:4). If you are drawn toward beauty, maybe you should consider the arts. As you open your mind to a vocation, you need to consider what makes your heart burn.

What kind of things do you learn quickly and easily? Perhaps you grasp the workings of a computer more rapidly than others do. While there is value in learning and training, by the time people are seriously looking for a vocation, their motor skills and mental operations have already developed patterns. In the quest for our calling we should consider what we naturally do well. Matthew is a dear friend of mine who is fluent in several languages and can read and interpret ancient languages as well. I don't know why, but he is just good at it. Matt also understands the language of computers and is a skilled computer technician. His love for God drew him into the ministry, and now his ministry usually involves creative and effective communication. Go figure.

Finally, ask yourself the question, "What activities give me a deep sense of satisfaction?" I know very few teachers who remain in education for the money. Undoubtedly, there are headaches and frustrations in education, but the transformation of young hearts and minds deeply satisfies the soul of a teacher. What kind of experiences and activities leave you feeling full, abundant, content?

Think about the inherent qualities you possess as well as the talents that have emerged in your character as you have grown from childhood to adulthood. Listen carefully to these voices because they just may complement or correspond to a divinely guided calling. In fact, not only do our beliefs and character qualities shape our calling; the Spirit imparts gifts that may speak to our potential vocation.

Question #3: What are my spiritual gifts?

Believers receive spiritual gifts when they surrender their lives to Christ. About spiritual gifts, Paul said, "All these are the work of one and the same Spirit, and he gives them to each one, just as he determines. The body is a unit, though it is made up of many parts; and though all its parts are many, they form one body. So it is with Christ. For we were all baptized by one Spirit into one body" (1 Corinthians 12:11–13).

And again to the church in Rome: "We have different gifts, according to the grace given us. If a man's gift is prophesying, let him use it in proportion to his faith. If it is serving, let him serve; if it is teaching, let him teach; if it is encouraging, let him encourage; if it is contributing to the needs of others, let him give generously; if it is leadership, let him govern diligently; if it is showing mercy, let him do it cheerfully" (Romans 12:6–8).

From the standpoint of our spiritual lives, we can see where we fit into the work of the local church and how our giftedness complements the kingdom of God. For the same reasons that we carefully consider our role of service in Christian ministry, we examine our giftedness for the purpose of our vocation—we want to make a meaningful contribution.

Sandy, a dear saint in my church, would pummel me weekly for a post in the work of the church. She was extremely outgoing, so, without considering her strengths and weaknesses, we gave her the job of greeting people as they came to church. Sandy faithfully arrived early, but she didn't just greet people as they came through the doors to worship—she assaulted them with conversation and testimonies. When one sweet woman admitted that her week hadn't gone well, Sandy scoured the Scriptures with her and pounded her with biblical insight.

I was dismayed. I'm all for Bible promises and Bible study and personal testimonies, but it became eminently clear that Sandy needed another post. So, I handed Sandy a spiritual gifts inventory. Upon completing it, she remarked, "I'm so glad you gave me this survey. I think I have the gift of evangelism!"

Spiritual gifts inventories don't tell you what your gift is; they orient you toward an area in which you should prayerfully experiment. The Spirit confirms the gifts He gives to the church, and Sandy was confirmed. She soon had small-group Bible studies several nights of the week. My church grew because of her efforts, and her spirit was at peace, with a new sense of belonging. Perhaps the personal contentment you get from discovering your spiritual gifts can aid in shaping the discovery of your vocation.

I love the story of the little boy who longed to get a part in the school play. He was very energetic and enthusiastic—so much so that his mother feared the director would reject him. On the way to the school for an audition, the little boy could barely stay in his seat, and his mom nervously bit her lip as he scampered into the building. When she arrived to pick him up after school, she feared she might meet a dejected child. Instead, he hopped and waved his way down the sidewalk and bounced into the car, speaking so fast that his mother couldn't understand a word he was saying. Finally, she calmed him down enough to hear his report. "I have a part in the school play!" he shouted. Then, eyes wide and grinning proudly from one ear to the other, he said, "I've been chosen to clap and cheer. The teacher thinks I'm the best at making lots of noise!"

Discovering what it means to live God's will for your life is more a journey than it is some striking revelation. This holds true when thinking about how you should spend forty-plus hours a week in your vocation. It is entirely possible that your calling will come to you as part of an ongoing process.

As you consider what your calling is, ruminate on what beliefs you hold that are not negotiable. Invite others to join you as you reflect on the qualities and talents that are unmistakably evident in your life. And determine what gifts God has given you to serve His church and reach His world with the gospel. Your personal makeup is inextricably tied to your spiritual identity and therefore can inform you as to your potential vocation.

The exchange and interaction with God on the road to wherever He is leading you is a trade—a trading of words, concerns, values, and wishes that unifies your purposes. As I have watched and listened to those who take joy in such a journey, I have noticed a few tips and tools they have used that you may find helpful. Many of these tools of the trade are simple and almost unnoticeable, but if you practice them faithfully, you will begin to hear voices.

Tool #1: Be willing to do the little things well every day.

I tend to become preoccupied with the big goal that extends well into the future, and I'm not alone. But the road to all great achievements has always been built on the substratum of many little successes.

Elgin Staples, a young man from the Midwest, served in World War II on the USS *Astoria*. Enemy fire hit the big ship, damaging it badly. Then a gun turret exploded, wounding Staples in both legs and throwing him into the water. The midshipman activated a trigger attached to a safety belt he wore around his waist, and the belt enabled him to float in the water.

Four hours later, another ship picked him up out of the water and returned him to the *Astoria*. The captain tried to save the ship by beaching it, but it sank instead. Back in the water again, Staples's lifebelt kept him afloat, saving him from certain death. He was one of five hundred rescued from the water by another ship, which carried them to safety.

On that ship, Staples examined the lifebelt that he had faithfully worn around his waist. He noticed that it had been manufactured by the Firestone Tire and Rubber Company; he recognized the label because his mother worked for Firestone. Staples also noticed a number attached to the belt. On home leave, he asked his mother about the number. She told him the company insisted that for the war effort, every employee must take the responsibility to inspect and certify that what they had made functioned properly.

Elgin Staples remembered the number he'd found on his lifebelt, so he repeated it to his mother. She smiled a knowing smile—the number was her personal code, which she affixed to every piece of equipment she inspected. Staples's mom went to work every day and quietly did her job, as menial as it may have seemed—and she did it faithfully. The fruit of such labor is rarely ever known, but in this case, the reward of doing the little things well was unmistakable.

Being willing to do the little things well every day is a biblical principle Paul referred to as "sowing and reaping." He claimed that we "reap what we sow." Don't allow yourself to become tired of doing your work well. Don't burn out on the little things, because the great things that come to us are borne on the backs of lots of little things. Paul was reminded of this principle in his own life. He said, "I planted the seed, Apollos watered it, but God made it grow" (1 Corinthians 3:6).

Tool #2: Become a lifelong learner.

While many adults in the workplace today are aware of the uncertainty of "lifelong careers," college students often think that their decision about a career is "for life." One student revealed her expectations about her year of service as a student missionary, saying, "I was hoping that teaching elementary school for a year would kind of help me decide what I wanted to do *for the rest of my life.*" I wondered, *Does she really believe that what she chooses to do in college is what she is destined to do for life?* I'm sure some people follow that path, but what enables anyone to stay on that path or choose another is a teachable spirit.

Have you ever noticed that the most effective and inspiring teachers are the ones most hungry to learn something new? I believe the other side of the spiritual gift of teaching is a desire to learn. I am aware of instructors who never change the content or character of their courses. What they learned long ago is good enough for today. Such teachers are least able to shape students positively. Lifelong learning is an approach to life. We should taste with wonder every morsel that an average day feeds us. If a co-worker annoys us, instead of shutting down and avoiding them, a teachable spirit will make us curious about what is wrong and how to make it right. Think back to the story of Jesus healing the boy who was born blind. The disciples asked a dead-end question, "Who sinned?" We might ask the question, "Why this innocent little boy?" " 'Neither this man nor his parents sinned,' said Jesus, 'but this happened so that the work of God might be displayed in his life. As long as it is day, we must do the work of him who sent me. Night is coming, when no one can work. While I am in the world, I am the light of the world' " (John 9:3–5).

I love how Jesus squeezed every situation to find every bit of insight into God's glory. In our trials and struggles, perhaps instead of asking the question *why*, we could be wondering *how* we might glorify God in the current circumstance. Lifelong learners rarely lack opportunities for new growth. Lifelong learners rarely run short of new horizons to pursue. Even when life smacks them around, those with a teachable spirit soar higher and discover other ways to go.

Tool #3: Be a thermostat instead of a thermometer.

A thermometer simply measures the temperature of the environment. A thermostat holds the standard for the ideal and switches on the resources necessary to achieve it. Whatever vocation you enter, think like a thermostat! Embracing all that God has revealed in His Word, all that you are good at, all that you have a desire to do, pool all your resources to make it happen. College is expensive, but if your goal requires that you have a degree, the question shifts from whether you can afford it to what you need to do to make it happen. Becoming a thermostat means finding a way. Paul called all believers to be thermostats with his timeless appeal, "Do not be conformed to this world, but be transformed by the renewal of your mind, that by testing you may discern what is the will of God, what is good, acceptable, and perfect" (Romans 12:2, ESV). Make no mistake, the challenge is huge, but God will provide His help; His blessings will be unmistakable.

Believe me, it is tempting just to let the world determine which options are obtainable and which are impossible. When Jesus happened upon a man sitting by the pool, He asked, " 'Do you want to be healed?' " (John 5:6, ESV). I completely understand the sick man's frustration. Adversity makes it is easy to feel powerless. When we lose control of one aspect of our life, we feel as though we've lost control of everything and become a slave to our circumstances. The sick man's response to Jesus makes it clear that he felt this way. He said, " 'Sir, I have no one to put me into the pool when the water is stirred up, and while I am going another steps down before me' " (verse 7, ESV). Jesus gave him an alternate route to healing that he hadn't thought of before, and he was healed.

When there seems to be no way to accomplish a task, either the task is utterly impossible or something is wrong with your vision. One year when I worked as a counselor at a summer camp, I was assigned six horrible, obnoxious, whiny boys. They wouldn't work as a team, and they belittled each other constantly. Their fighting and bickering became unbearable; so I did the only thing I thought would work with boys—I took them out in the woods and challenged their emerging manhood. I said, "I brought you here to do what no other group has been able to do yet." They were listening, so I continued to goad them: "I'm sure this is a waste of time, but the goal is to build a fort out of the elements of the forest while being handicapped in one way or another." At this point, I waved some ropes and blindfolds.

"Ah, this is stupid," one of the boys chided.

I immediately agreed, "Yeah, forget about it. I'll try one of the girls' cabins."

That did it. Though the amount of testosterone brewing in those young boys was minimal, it was enough to move them into battle. I tied the hands of two boys, leaving their eyes and feet free. I tied the feet of two boys, leaving their hands and eyes free. And I blindfolded two boys, leaving their hands and feet free. Then I said, "There's no way you guys can do this in two hours, so don't hurt yourself trying."

During the first hour and a half, I witnessed frightening acts of foolish effort. One of the boys threw a limb to another boy, saying, "This will make a good roof support." Unfortunately, he threw it to one of his cabin-mates who had been blindfolded. When that boy had recovered, they all began to talk, and then, like water finding its way downhill, they began to cooperate. In minutes, they were working efficiently. The two boys whose feet were tied remained in one place, for they could see and use their hands to build the fort. The boys who were blindfolded carried wood, rocks, and branches while being guided by boys who could walk and see but whose hands were tied. They didn't finish the fort in those two hours, but every day throughout the week they returned to the site, traded handicaps, and continued to build it.

Thermostats, not thermometers.

Tool #4: Be fearless with your ambition and fluid with your itinerary.

I have interviewed numerous individuals who have allowed God to guide them through a Voice they heard in their heart and through the circumstances of their daily life. They seem to agree about vocation:

- We are gifted and passionate in various ways, so God's will embraces many vocations. Choose prayerfully, sincerely, and earnestly.
- Being willing to learn fortifies us for the greater challenges ahead. As John C. Maxwell says in the book *Failing Forward*, "The difference between average people and achieving people is their perception of and response to failure."[8]
- We need to articulate to ourselves the connection between what we believe and our sense of calling and how they can be expressed in the career we choose.

Holly's journey embodies the fearless and fluid pilgrimage of being true to one's vocation. She entered the nursing field enjoying the challenge of medical service and the flexible schedule. Then the legal aspects of her job fascinated her, so she seized the opportunity to work as a nurse-consultant for a law firm. As she did so, she discovered an emerging desire to write the motions and argue the cases in court.

Most people I know who enter into a career in nursing aren't thinking, *I wonder if this will lead to a career in law?* But Holly fearlessly entered the ranks of law students and completed her law degree. While her experience in civil law was meaningful, opportunities to practice criminal law energized her. Then the work she did as a prosecutor led to yet another opportunity for public service—as a judge. Holly sensed in each phase of her vocational journey that God was affirming the myriad gifts and talents He bestowed on her, as He does in each of us.

God gave us the mind-set to work. Whether that means raising a household of children or starting a small business, God wants to fill our lives with His purpose. If God desperately needs you to be a prophet, He will set ablaze the next juniper bush you walk by as He did with Moses. If you see a burning bush and God isn't speaking to you through it, put the fire out before it spreads to something else—and in the meantime, reflect on the gifts God has given you.

What do you really want to do? Can you do what you really want to do and glorify God without compromise? What do you do well? What kinds of tasks come easily to you? What kind of work scares you but intrigues you at the same time? What do others you love and trust say about your character? What skills do you have?

You have to launch out into something to pay the bills. But beware: Fishermen become church planters, nurses become judges, and some light up their world while remaining in the same vocation all their life.

---

1. Michael Green, ed., *1500 Illustrations for Biblical Preaching* (Grand Rapids, Mich.: Baker Books, 1989), 396.

2. Troy Fitzgerald, *The Student Missionary Experience and Its Impact on Young Adults* (Ph.D. diss., Andrews University, 2005), 52, 53.

3. Bob Reccord and Randy Singer, *Made to Count* (Nashville, Tenn.: W Publishing Group, 2004), xiii.

4. Po Bronson, *What Should I Do With My Life?* (New York: Random House, 2003), xiii.

5. Ibid.

6. Charles S. Spurgeon, "A Well-Ordered Life," sermon no. 878, delivered 6/27/1869 at the Metropolitan Tabernacle, Newington; http://www.spurgeongems.org/vols13-15/chs878.pdf.

7. Marcus Buckingham and Donald O. Clifton, *Now, Discover Your Strengths* (New York: The Free Press, 2001), 75.

8. John C. Maxwell, *Failing Forward* (Nashville, Tenn.: Thomas Nelson Publishers, 2000), 2.

Questions for Reflection

1. When in your journey have you wrestled with the fear of failure? How does our deep need to be successful shape our view of God's will for our life?

2. What is the basic difference between a career and a calling? What is your personal experience with the tension that exists between trying to reconcile your abilities with what you sense God is calling you to do?

3. Some have suggested that balance is the secret of living the abundant life. What is the difference between striving for balance and seeking the well-ordered life?

4. Which question in the section "Questions to Ask Yourself" seems to be most relevant to you at this stage in your journey?

5. In what way do you see God at work in the career you are choosing?

6. Name someone, if you can, whom God has guided into a calling that differs from his or her career. Name someone whom God has guided into a career that is his or her calling.

Chapter 7

You've Got the Right One, Baby!

Julia and I, newlyweds, meandered through a crowded mall with no real agenda. She entered a picture-frame shop, and I decided to check out the cookie vendor directly across from it. I completed my purchase before she did, so I loitered in the mall, watching the shoppers as my new bride made her way to the checkout line. I remember looking at her and thinking, *I'm either blessed or lucky—probably both.*

However, my blessing turned to a curse and my luck took a turn for the worse as my beloved bride strode from the store and grabbed the hand of a young man standing just outside it. She then lurched forward, locking her eyes on the next retail target a few doors away and dragging the man with her.

My shock and pain turned to uncontrollable laughter as Julia marched the stranger down the mall and he walked along with my wife, slightly embarrassed but mostly amused. When Julia finally looked at the stranger to whom she was clinging, she dropped his arm in horror (that had to affect the poor guy adversely) and apologized. Then she scanned the area quickly and found me holding a large chocolate chip cookie in one hand and waving with the other while simultaneously wiping tears of laughter from my eyes. Marriage has its moments—some of them highly amusing!

Throughout this book, my emphasis has been on walking with God—I've said that guidance becomes a byproduct of our relationship with Him. God does guide us into relationships that potentially lead to marriage. His will, however, may have more to do with choosing *rightly* the person to marry than with choosing the right person to marry. This chapter contains a few reality checkpoints along the way to finding God's will for marriage.

Checkpoint #1: The search for the perfect match is a deceptive endeavor.

One of the myths I discussed early in this book is the popular assumption that God has a specific plan for each of us—meaning a specific job, a specific place to live, and a specific person to marry. I don't believe it works that way. The idea of choosing the right person suggests that only one or perhaps a select few are right for us, which means that we'd better not make a mistake or we might miss out on God's will. It also implies that the perfect person—the other person—should be the one doing the adapting and adjusting. Everything depends on whether that person possesses the right recipe of attributes to complement ours.

I believe instead that we should take responsibility for becoming the kind of person who would make a godly partner in marriage. Rather than focusing on making the right match, we should seek to become the right material for marriage: faithful, honest, loving, considerate, supportive, selfless, giving, and so forth. We can't control or change another person's character, habits, and perceptions, but we can be responsible for our own.

Furthermore, how well we know another person is so fluid and immeasurable. Think of the person who knows you best, and ask yourself, "How much about me do they *really* know?" Can you reveal to another human being even 2 percent of all the thoughts, the emotions, the experiences, and the responses you've ever had? And is it possible that we enable others to know us only as we invest ourselves in committed relationships? So, the context of committed relationships provides the most effective environment in which to discover who people really are and whether they are "a good match" for us.

Checkpoint #2: We can fall head over heels in love with a person we should never marry.

Just because we fall in love doesn't mean God has blessed our choice of a mate. All it means is that we are human. Conventional wisdom claims that "birds of a feather" should "flock together." Many marriages that were perfect matches of people with shared interests have fallen apart. The idea that "opposites attract" is also popular, but marriages that were born out of a curious attraction to a totally different personality also fail.

God's Word offers an enduring formula in the form of a warning that many try to ignore or reinterpret: "Do not be yoked together with unbelievers. For what do righteousness and wickedness have in common? Or what fellowship can light have with darkness? What harmony is there between Christ and Belial? What does a believer have in common with an unbeliever?" (2 Corinthians 6:14, 15). Robert Jeffress unpacks the meaning behind how we are "yoked," stating, "The phrase *bound together* carries the idea of two unequal animals, such as an ox and a donkey, being harnessed together to perform a task. The ox pulls against the donkey and the donkey works against the ox, resulting in constant friction and an ultimate stalemate."[1]

I often wonder why so many people discover after marriage that their spiritual values are incongruent with those of their spouse. Apparently, many people blatantly ignore how unequal their foundations are. It may be that young adults simply don't articulate those values to each other prior to marriage. People can marry without reflecting on the bedrock values and assumptions that undergird their perspectives. Admittedly, people forge some of their beliefs in the fire of marriage, but an equally yoked marriage deepens our commitments, whereas an unequally yoked marriage nags us to compromise our beliefs to keep the peace.

Checkpoint #3: A soul mate is not someone we find but someone we become.

The story is told of a couple who went on a date to celebrate the fortieth anniversary of their marriage. When they returned home, they sat across from each other at the kitchen table as they had each night for years, and the husband put some bread in the toaster—a heel and a piece from the center of the loaf—as was their evening ritual. When the toast popped up, the man buttered both pieces, handed the heel to his wife, and kept the other piece for himself.

Forty years of frustration over this simple act finally came to a head, and the wife broke down in tears. Her husband couldn't understand why she was crying; he pleaded with her to tell him what he'd done wrong. She looked at him and wailed, "I can't understand why you always give me the heel. I *hate* the heel. For forty years, I've had to eat the heel of the bread because you want a center piece for yourself. That's selfish!"

The man looked in astonishment at the toast sitting on the plates, and then tears welled up in his eyes. "Honey," he said, "for years I've given you the heel because I think it's the best part. I thought you liked it too. I'm so sorry."

No matter how much you think you know someone, there will always be more to learn about that person.

God's will for marriage is that a man and a woman would grow together as one. Paul used the analogy in Ephesians, saying that as a man and a woman become one in marriage, so Christ and the church are to become one in mission. But becoming soul mates is a process. Note what God says about marriage: " 'A man shall leave his father and his mother, and be joined to his wife; and they shall become one flesh' " (Genesis 2:24, NASB). What many don't understand is that this dynamic doesn't happen immediately. It happens over time, by living through life's varying experiences together. We might compare it to planting two trees side by side. As the roots extend out, they intertwine with each other, and over the seasons, the two trees eventually share one root system. Aboveground, the two trunks stand separate, but underground, they are united as one.

We commonly hear someone say, "She is my soul mate" or "I found the perfect guy; we are soul mates." But a soul mate is someone who becomes embedded in your personhood and you into his or hers. The goals and struggles of life shape the two of you, binding you together and making the unit you've formed stronger than either of you would be alone. Instead of draining each other's convictions, you spur each other on to even deeper devotion. No one is likely to argue with you when you introduce your spouse as your soul mate. Just be aware that the kind of unity the Bible pictures in the marriage covenant doesn't result from choosing the perfect person. It is the outgrowth of perfect trust and enduring commitment to each other over the seasons.

Checkpoint #4: Love is NOT all we need.

According to John Lennon, "all you need is love." But I believe we need more. Because there is some confusion about the meaning of the word *love*, you might wait for a clearer definition before you bank all your hopes on it. I'm not trying to be sacrilegious, but with the rock group Foreigner singing "I want to know what love is" and Howard Jones asking, "What is love, anyway?" I wonder if love might be *too* illusive.

Ninety percent of the population believes that *being in love* is what makes a good marriage. One of my favorite marriage resources reports some interesting research about our perceptions of the word *love*. "When asked to list the essential ingredients of love as a basis for marriage, . . . a survey of more than a thousand college students revealed that, 'no single item was mentioned by at least one half of those responding.' In other words, we can't agree on what love is. Or perhaps, more accurately, we don't *know* what love is."[2]

When you stand at the altar looking dreamily into the eyes of the love of your life and saying, "I love you," are you sure you know what you mean by that? Do you understand fully what the other person means by saying that? I can honestly say that I love my wife, Julia, and that I am still in love with her. But I don't love perfectly or consistently. In fact, my ability to love is often far from what I believe and wish for in myself.

Not only are our expressions of love imperfect, but sometimes we make it hard for others to love us. Can the perfect plan God has for marriage rest fully on love? Perhaps we should consider what Dietrich Bonhoeffer wrote about the relationship between love and marriage:

> Marriage is more than your love for each other. It has a higher dignity and power, for it is God's holy ordinance, through which he wills to perpetuate the human race till the end of time. In your love you see only your two selves in the world, but in marriage you are a link in the chain of the generations, which God causes to come and to pass away to his glory, and calls into his kingdom. As high as God is above man, so high are the sanctity, the rights, and the promise of marriage above the sanctity, the rights, and the promise of love. It is not your love that sustains the marriage, but from now on, the marriage that sustains your love.[3]

So, we need to understand what we mean when we say, "I'll marry you." The whole idea of marriage began at Creation. At that time, "the LORD God said, 'It is not good for the man to be alone. I will make a helper suitable for him' " (Genesis 2:18). And the plan of marriage took shape as God announced that men should leave their father and mother and be united to their wife, and " 'they will become one flesh' " (verse 24). The holiness and perfection of the marriage covenant provides what

I call "a greenhouse for love to grow." It is important to know what we mean when we say, "I love you." We need love, but it isn't all we need. Marriage requires commitment.

God's loving ways

The success of marriage may depend on how well people mirror the way God demonstrates His love to humanity. I would draw your attention away from the volumes of clichés and catchphrases about relationships and simply examine God's loving ways. As we are mindful of the way God loves us, we will be better equipped to love each other the way God designed people to love.

First, God looks beyond the price tag of love and sees the value of loving. The cost of loving humanity was high, but to Him it was worth it. Romans 5:8 says, "While we were yet sinners Christ died for us" (NASB). Even when we were at our worst, God did what was best. If you want to mirror God's loving ways, don't let the cost of living and loving each other distract you from the ultimate value of marriage. It's worth it. Make no mistake, it *is* expensive. It'll cost you your pride, your need to be right, your place in line. Marriage is expensive—but it's worth the cost. You can experience God's loving ways by making your relationship with your marriage partner more valuable than anything else on earth.

Second, God knows how to put people in their place. From the beginning of time, God has offered us the seat of honor by making us in His image. Even when humanity chose to aim low, God promised to put us in a high place. We are blessed, honored, cherished, and incredibly valued creatures—above all else. If God has shown us anything, it is the way to believe the best about another person. Make no mistake, it is hard sometimes to put people in their proper place. But we can practice God's loving ways by putting the one we marry in the place of honor. Can you imagine the happiness generated in a home where members of the family treat each other as God has destined them to be?

And finally, consider the loving way God conveys His feelings toward people. He is not only creative but also comprehensive in the way He communicates His love. Hebrews 1 says that God has spoken to us many ways, but today He speaks through Jesus, who is the exact representation of God Himself. That's right. God doesn't just find clever ways to say "I love you"—He finds a way to say it in everything He does.

As I look at reports showing that people are waiting longer and longer before they marry, I wonder what is prompting this change. Frankly, I think that most young adults consider the whole idea of intimacy and companionship attractive. I also think marriage is the one thing they don't want to fail at. Combine the anxiety about messing up in marriage with the myth that the divorce rate is at 50 percent, and it's no wonder that young adults are a bit tentative.

I want to dispel the notion that divorce is as popular as marriage. In 2003, for every thousand people, there were 7.5 marriages and 3.8 divorces filed. But comparing the number of divorces with the number of marriages is terribly misleading. The number of couples getting divorced comes from the massive pool containing everyone who has ever been married and is still living. It is safe to say there are far more marriages that make it in this world than marriages that fail. *The New York Times* reports, "Studies find that the divorce rate in the United States has never reached one in every two marriages, and new research suggests that, with rates now declining, it probably never will."[4] The bottom line is that marriage is a rich, meaningful part of God's plan for our lives.

But not everyone should or must enter into marriage. Paul affirmed those for whom marriage isn't part of their journey, and he says that he himself has chosen to remain single (see 1 Corinthians 7:7, 8). Many people lead rich, meaningful lives as singles, and they possess a perspective on God's will that is helpful and inspiring.

God places a high premium on relationships when He describes our union with Him in terms of marriage. He also likens the moments in history when His people were rebellious and unfaithful to Him to divorce. In both descriptions, the common element is intimacy. In marriage, there is the celebration of intimacy, and in separation, there is the betrayal of intimacy. So, as your journey leads you to relationships that may potentially lead to marriage, remember that the guidance that you so desired when making decisions is available as you walk with and cling to God in an abiding, obedient relationship with the Savior.

1. Robert Jeffress, *Hearing the Master's Voice* (Colorado Springs, Colo.: WaterBrook Press, 2001), 143.

2. Les Parrot III and Leslie Parrott, *Saving Your Marriage Before It Starts* (Grand Rapids, Mich.: Zondervan, 1995), 31.

3. Dietrich Bonhoeffer, "A Wedding Sermon from Prison"; http://preachingtoday.com/32781. (Note: This is a membership site.)

4. Dan Hurley, "Divorce Rates: It's Not as High as You Think," *The New York Times*, April 19, 2005.

Questions for Reflection

1. Do you think God guides people to the perfect person for them to marry?

2. This chapter contains the statement "A soul mate is not someone you find but someone you become." Do you agree or disagree with that statement? Why?

3. Think of several people you know very well whose definition of love might vary significantly. To what degree do you think we know what others mean when they say, "I love you"?

4. Dietrich Bonhoeffer claimed, "It is not your love that sustains the marriage, but from now on, the marriage that sustains your love." Who do you know that personifies this statement? How has their relationship been a source of inspiration to you?

5. In what way does God's love for humanity become a textbook for learning to love someone else?

Chapter 8

Trail Tips for Starting Today

Let's review some of the principles for discovering God's will:

- God has a plan for you, and His plan is good.
- God's greatest desire—greater than finding you a particular job, place to live, or person to marry—is to walk with you.
- Knowing God's will is primarily a matter of knowing Him. God's guidance is a byproduct of a walking, living relationship with Him.
- Don't let what you don't know confuse you about what you do know.
- Don't let what you can see obscure what has been revealed to you.
- Don't let your aspirations distract you from doing what you should do today.
- Don't let the cost of doing God's will make you forget its value.
- God has spoken plainly in His Word about what He wants for you. Deliberately begin living the will clearly revealed in His Word, and God will guide you one step at a time.
- Because we're human, our wills naturally conflict with God's will. Therefore, praying "not my will but Yours be done" becomes a journey rather than simply a matter of praying one prayer.
- When adversity strikes, as Scripture tells us it will, find a place to stand where God can hang on to you. Then you and your story will strengthen someone else along the way.
- Walk with God as you discover your vocation. Then your journey with all its successes and failures will make you rich.

• God's plan for marriage parallels His desire to be one with you.

Discovering God's will is not a program but an approach to life. Consequently, living God's plan for your life means learning to walk with God. It is a learning experience. In fact, Moses spoke to God as a "man speaks to his friend," yet the great prophet of Israel appealed to God, saying, "If you are pleased with me, *teach me your ways* so I may know you and continue to find favor with you" (Exodus 33:13; emphasis added). David echoed the same desire, singing,

> *Teach me your way*, O LORD,
>   and I will walk in your truth;
> give me an undivided heart,
>   that I may fear your name (Psalm 86:11, emphasis added).

The man who spoke to God face to face and the man after God's own heart both referred to God's guidance as something we *learn*, not something we *see*.

At a county fair, a local artist demonstrated how to make pottery from a lump of clay on a pottery wheel. I distinctly remember thinking to myself, *I can do that*—though, clearly, adding just the right amount of water while manipulating the lump of clay that spun on the wheel required a certain knack. People who hang around and watch intently risk becoming "volunteers." I soon discovered that watching an artist make clay pots doesn't teach you how to do it yourself. Teaching is more than telling, and knowing is more than hearing information. We learn what God's will is experientially, and today is the only time you can begin.

Every Palm Pilot and Daytimer has a place where a person can make a list of things to do. I like the notepads that read "Things to Do Today." The "today" is important because many of us tend to procrastinate—especially when the things to do aren't easy. The "today" is also crucial because if we're not careful, things that demand our immediate attention may fill our day. The Bible says, "Exhort one another every day, as long as it is called 'today,' that none of you may be hardened by the deceitfulness of sin" (Hebrews 3:13, ESV). The saying is true, "Don't put off till tomorrow what you can do today."

I suggest that you begin the day with some basic activities that deepen your relationship with God as well as your impact on the people around you. This will get the wheels of your search turning. Earlier, we noted how hard it is to turn a car when the vehicle isn't moving. Remember: As you move through each today, Jesus will travel with you.

Activity #1: Knowing God's will is really about knowing God (see John 17:3–5), so have a conversation with Him.

Often, our prayers barely go beyond the burrito we're asking God to bless. If you want the God of heaven to guide you, take time to connect with Him in such a way that you get to know Him better. When we seek to become acquainted with people, we examine the qualities we see in their behavior. We listen to their stories and compare them to our own experience.

I took a young man to lunch, and as we sat down with our trays full of food, we both bowed our heads to pray—except he pushed his tray forward. I didn't think much of it, but after I had thanked God for my food, I looked up and he was still praying. I waited and waited and continued to wait for four minutes. I couldn't believe it. How rude! The moment he opened his eyes and lifted up his head, he smiled, grabbed his tray, pulled it back in front of him, and started to eat. I just stared at him. Then, with a mouth full of burrito, he said, "What?"

"What's up with the five-minute prayer? Are you trying to look more spiritual than me?"

He explained that he had often prayed more for his food than for the things that really mattered in his life. So now when he eats, instead of praying for his food, he pushes his tray forward and talks to God about the things that are most important to him.

When Jesus was teaching the disciples to pray, He said, "When you pray, go into your room, *close the door* and pray to your Father" (Matthew 6:6; emphasis added). Close the door because a conversation with God can transform your day, if not your life.

Activity #2: Expect great things to happen to you today.

Teachers know that their expectations strongly influence how their students perform. The Master Teacher, Jesus, said to His disciples, " 'I tell you the truth, anyone who has faith in me will do what I have been doing. He will do even greater things than these, because I am going to the Father' " (John 14:12). This might seem hard to believe at first, but consider the thousands of people who came to know Jesus when the Holy Spirit finally got hold of Peter. We miss many great moments in the day simply because we don't anticipate that they are possible, not to mention probable. Bruce Wilkinson illustrated the impact of low expectations with the following story:

In 1900 the Census Bureau bought a new type of tabulating machine for its workers. It estimated that employees could type in 550 cards a day with the new machines. After a couple of weeks there was a great deal of emotional distress, and the director of the census was forced to conclude that he couldn't require 550 a day. So workers began to average many fewer cards a day. About a month later, the bureau found it needed more workers to do all the work that wasn't getting done. Due to the lack of room, however, the new employees were put in a different building. These workers were taught how to use the machines, but weren't told how many cards were expected of them. When the ceiling was removed and the sky became the limit, workers processed an average of 2,100 cards a day with no aches, pains or complaints. Such is the power of expectations.[1]

If you desire to live God's will for your life today, try shifting your "gray" expectations to great expectations. Do you expect that God will cause you to cross paths with someone who is searching for hope? Do you expect God to use your words, your skills, and your interests to bless someone in need? This doesn't mean you won't have days that seem unproductive or frustrating, but it does mean that you will be looking for opportunities you would never see unless you were anticipating them. Expect great things from your day today.

Activity #3: Engage in what you already know is God's will for you.

Whenever the stories and sayings of Scripture start to feel ordinary to me, I read the testimony John wrote near the end of his Gospel about how he came to write it. First, let me note that John says that in addition to the stories he's told, "Jesus did many other things as well. If every one of them were written down, I suppose that even the whole world would not have room for the books that would be written" (John 21:25). Now, as to why John wrote what he did: "These are written that you may believe that Jesus is the Christ, the Son of God, and that by believing you may have life in his name" (20:31). It is safe to say that not everything you want to know is in the Bible—but everything God wants you to know is there.

As you face a new today, consider responding to God's revealed will in the Bible. In chapter 3, we discussed six things God wishes for His children:

1. God's will is that we receive salvation (Ephesians 1:11, 12; Matthew 18:12–14; 2 Peter 3:8, 9).

2. God's will is that we grow (Colossians 1:9–12; 4:12, 13; 1 Thessalonians 4:3–6).

3. God's will is that we be filled with His Spirit (Ephesians 5:17–21).

4. God's will is that we work for others with a servant's heart (Ephesians 6:5–8).

5. God's will is that we quiet the critics with acts of goodness (1 Peter 2:15, 16).

6. God's will for us is an abundant life (1 Thessalonians 5:16–18).

What do you think would happen if you chose to focus on one item of the six each day? Perhaps one day you could keep in your purse or wallet a picture of Calvary, reminding you of the gift of eternal life through Christ's sacrifice. Every Monday you might choose to start your week with acts of goodness to the person who annoys you the most. Living God's wish list is a life-transforming experience. Can you imagine working with someone who lived like this? Keep in mind that the more general your response, the more you will wonder whether you actually followed through or not, so be specific. For example, if the portion of God's will you intend to focus on today is that God wants you to grow, choose one specific quality you know God wants you to work on in your life.

I know that God wants me to be more patient with my family, so today I'm going to practice patience with my youngest boy, Morgan, who doesn't know what time is. I'll try not to hurry the little guy when we're getting ready for school, when we stop to look at bugs on the sidewalk on the way home, and when it's time to put toys away. Now I have a plan. Does it seem too simplistic? You'll never convince me that it is because as I focused on those three little moments, my heart soared with a sense of victory and joy.

I dare you to become deliberate regarding God's will. I dare you to be specific with the way you apply yourself to God's wish list. Those who try to implement these six wishes on God's list won't short-circuit about not knowing which job to take.

Activity #4: Take time today to look in the mirror and reflect on the ways that God has guided you in the past.

What do you see when you take time to reflect? You might see people who have been pivotal in your journey. You might see events that have shaped the way you perceive God and the potential of your life. You may even remember choices you regret or opportunities that you missed. But the exercise of reflection strengthens our ability to see more than what is immediately before us. Reflection opens a library of experiences that can assist us in the choices we make today and tomorrow. Reflection deepens our heart and grows our mind. Reflection teaches us to allow our regrets to heal instead of to cripple us. Reflection transforms our failures into firsthand experiences that make us wiser. Reflective people hear God's voice in ways that people who live fast and furiously never will.

Get a journal or keep a digital log—but whatever you do, in a concrete way chronicle the events of your journey, noting the little things you learn as well as the monumental ones. In some of the discipleship materials I've written, I've tended to get into a wrestling match with the designers because of my desire to have blank areas on the pages where people can write. People need a place to doodle, draw, and describe what is happening to them as well as what they long to have occur in their hearts. The designers would often argue that empty space is wasted space, but I disagree (and some designers do as well). The space is not empty; it is deliberately reserved for people to mark the salient points of their journey.

So design your day with space to write, think, reflect, and dream. Use planned moments for self-examination. Deepen your sensitivity to God's touch. Scan the Scriptures, and you will find fellow travelers who wire time into their life—time to reflect. Jesus is probably the best example. Even after unbelievably hard days, He stole away quietly to be alone. It might be the hardest activity to integrate into your day, but you will rarely feel empty if you take time to reflect.

Activity #5: Check your I.D. and remember who you are.

Daily check with God to assure yourself of who you really are. The world will scream aloud the ways you fall short. Part of living God's will for your life means seeing yourself the way He sees you. If you were to read everything God says about what He sees in you, you might be shocked. The Bible says

- You are a child of God (1 John 3:1, 22).
- "You are A CHOSEN RACE, A royal PRIESTHOOD, A HOLY NATION, A PEOPLE FOR God's OWN POSSESSION" (1 Peter 2:9, NASB).
- "You are all sons of light and sons of day" (1 Thessalonians 5:5).
- "You also, as living stones, are being built up as a spiritual house for a holy priesthood" (1 Peter 2:5, NASB).
- " 'You are the salt of the earth' " (Matthew 5:13).
- " 'You are the light of the world' " (Matthew 5:14).

- "You are Christ's body, and individually members of it" (1 Corinthians 12:27, NASB).
- "We are His workmanship, created in Christ Jesus for good works" (Ephesians 2:10, NASB).
- "You are no longer strangers and aliens, but you are fellow citizens with the saints, and are of God's household" (Ephesians 2:19, NASB).
- "We are ambassadors for Christ" (2 Corinthians 5:20, NASB).

The story is told of a melancholy lawyer who moved to a new place to begin a new law practice. Townspeople often observed him walking by himself in the evening with his head bowed and his whole posture deflated.

One day the lawyer confessed to an artist that in the past he had made a critical mistake that he'd never been able to shake. The artist said nothing, but a few weeks later, he invited the dejected lawyer to view a portrait in his studio. When the lawyer looked at the painting, he was surprised to see that it pictured him—only in the portrait, he stood tall and confident, with his head held high and ambition, vision, and courage written all over his face. The artist's portrayal of what he could be birthed a new vision in his heart. The lawyer said to himself, "If the artist can see that in me, then I can see it too. If he thinks that I can be that man, then I *will* be that man."

Activity #6: Both God and the devil are in the details, so choose wisely.

Some go too far when they assume that God handles the big picture but that people should make the little choices of life on their own. The problem with this line of thinking is that it runs contrary to Scripture. Paul wrote, "Continue to work out your salvation with fear and trembling, for it is God who works in you to will and to act according to his good purpose" (Philippians 2:12, 13). It seems to me this indicates that all of our daily life should be a cooperative venture. We've heard the saying, "The devil is in the details," but so God is there too. Will He guide you to buy the right home? Does He lead people through menial problems like finding their way to the highway when they get lost? When you're buying a car or baking a cake—is God willing to be involved in the minutia? Consider a few tips for getting God involved in the details of your life:

1. Talk to God directly and specifically about your situation, and remind Him that you're aware that He is near and knows what you are facing.

2. Claim the promise in James 4:8: "Come near to God and he will come near to you." In her book *The Great Controversy*, Ellen White assured us that our compassionate Savior "is as willing to listen to the prayer of faith [today] as when He walked visibly among men. The natural cooperates with the supernatural. It is a part of God's plan to grant us, in answer to the prayer of faith, that which He would not bestow did we not thus ask."[2]

3. Explain to God what you perceive to be the best way to handle the challenge you face, and invite Him to show you otherwise by any means He deems appropriate.

4. Take the steps you think are best in the full awareness that God is standing by your side. If you are honest with God about your willingness to go another direction, then He will show you, lead you, or inspire in that way—provided you are paying attention.

These conversations with God aren't abnormal or inappropriate, especially when you talk with Him frequently throughout the day.

One winter's night while I was living in Michigan, I went sledding. When I was ready to pack up and return home, I realized I had lost my keys somewhere in the snow in an area about seventy yards long and thirty-five yards wide. Complicating the matter, snow had been falling like manna all night.

My first thought was, *There is no way I'm even going to try to find those keys.* My second thought was, *I have to find those keys; they're the only set I own.* So, my fellow sledder, my little boy, and I prayed. At first I felt ridiculous to be asking God to help me find my keys. But as I prayed, what seemed like an awkward request became quite natural.

On that snowy Michigan hill, I followed the process I've noted above, saying, "Lord, You know I know the only way to start my car is with my keys. They're hidden somewhere in the snow. I'm willing to stay out here all night looking if that is the only way. I can call a locksmith, but You and I both know how expensive that is. Either way, I would like Your help. So guide me in my search through the snow, as impossible as finding those keys seems, I know You can help. If there is another way, show me and I will do it."

After I prayed, my boy and I started to scratch at the snow where we'd been sledding. I took a snow shovel and skimmed the top of the snow near the jump we had made for our sleds, and my shovel snagged and scratched on metal. Sure enough, it was my keys. Hallelujah!

A similar problem arose at another point in my journey when I left my keys in the ignition of my car and locked the doors. I prayed the same prayer, and ended up calling a locksmith. In both scenarios, I believe that God was with me. He was right there in the details and in all the expense and inconvenience incurred when the situation didn't work out the way I drew it up. I still believe making friends with the locksmith was a seed planted in the grand scheme of things. (To be continued in the next activity.)

Activity #7: Be mindful that you play a role in the sowing, watering, and reaping process of life.

Frank, the locksmith in the story above, never asked for Bible studies, but we had a good chat, and I extended my appreciation for his prompt and honest service to me. It is likely that your service to others plants a seed that will bear fruit in time. Sometimes the daily grind of service can wear you out, especially if your kindness goes unnoticed or unappreciated. Paul appealed to the church, "Let us not become weary in doing good, for at the proper time we will reap a harvest if we do not give up" (Galatians 6:9). Even Paul, with all his success, had to admit that his work was only part of a greater phenomenon. In the letter to the Corinthians, Paul said, "I planted the seed, Apollos watered it, but God made it grow" (1 Corinthians 3:6).

A community member had donated hundreds of tulip bulbs to a RAK team I had started. (A RAK team is a group of teenagers who do Random Acts of Kindness. We went out once a week and searched for opportunities to do something kind for someone in need.) It was fall, so we were going to plant the bulbs secretly in front yards of unsuspecting people while they were out. However, everyone seemed to be home—except Jenny, a sweet older woman who lived on her own and who was a member of the local church.

Michelle, a girl who had joined us for the first time, diligently planted bulbs in Jenny's front yard. She felt good about it, but spring was a long time away. And, unfortunately, in the meantime, Michelle disengaged. She got caught up in the wrong crowd and became distracted by some pretty meaningless things.

When springtime came, Jenny's yard was a magical display of tulips. It was pretty ostentatious—I think most of the three hundred tulip bulbs had ended up in her yard. One day, Michelle drove by with a bunch of friends. She saw the glory, remembered the joy she felt serving with the RAK team, and longed for the sense of purpose that she had experienced but that had seemed to ebb away. Her life seemed empty compared to what she had known before.

The tulips haunted Michelle every time she drove by Jenny's yard. Then, as spring made its way into summer, I noticed that Michelle was sitting in church with Jenny. Apparently, she grew tired of empty living, visited sweet little Jenny, and they became friends.

We never know what role each act of service plays in the grand scheme of things. Those who choose to live God's will for their life become part of a great work of sowing, watering, and reaping.

Slogans to adopt

"All for one." Living God's will for your life begins with a covenant—an agreement between you and God. Make a covenant with Him about your willingness to do His will, and make a list of things to do today to integrate living His will into everyday life.

The three musketeers are famous for their motto "All for one and one for all." Embedded deep in their hearts was the belief that the universe held something bigger than the ordinary for their lives. They had made a commitment to an ideal: honor. Christ made a similar challenge to those who would follow Him, saying, " 'Seek first his kingdom and his righteousness, and all these things will be given to you as well' " (Matthew 6:33). Everything will seem in disarray until something becomes first, best, and most in your life. Christ promises that if you begin with a commitment to His kingdom (a commitment to seeing His will be done on earth as it is in heaven), the other concerns of life will be manageable.

I'll never forget the look on Gina's face or the tone of joy in her voice when she told me that a simple shift transformed her whole life. Gina was a real estate agent who had begun to wonder why her life felt so anemic. She professed to be a Christian, but she rarely allowed her faith in God anywhere near her work—or her life, for that matter.

In her emptiness, Gina picked up God's Word and read, hoping to hear directly from Jesus. And she did. When she happened upon His challenge, "Seek first the kingdom of God and His righteousness," the words struck conviction to her heart. "I told God I would clear my schedule in the morning and begin seeking," she says, and she did. Gina drove up and down the streets of her community, praying for the people. The thought of the families who would be moving into town from far away and those who would be leaving to go elsewhere roused a commitment to help them in their journey. Gina's sales have remained the same. But each day she takes "the long way to work." And as she journeys through her town, she speaks to God about her people and her part in their journey.

"All in." I'm not a poker fan, but I know that the phrase "all in" signifies that the player isn't holding any resources back. The player is betting everything on his or her current hand. Usually this occurs at the end of the game, when the player is either desperately seeking to stay alive or believes his or her hand is unbeatable and is worth the risk of betting everything on it to win. God promises through the prophet Jeremiah, " 'You will seek me and find me when you seek me with all your heart' " (Jeremiah 29:13). God isn't suggesting a commitment of part of our life for part of a day. He calls for devotion, not devotions. Imagine if during your wedding ceremony, your would-be spouse were to announce, "I'm totally committed to this marriage and to you—except on Mondays." Absurd? With God, we need to go all in.

The trust-fall exercise captures the essence of going all in. During an outdoor team-building program, Kim stood on a six-foot-high platform with her back turned toward two lines of teammates. They were facing each other with their arms extended like a net, waiting to catch her. The idea was that she trusted them enough to fall backwards into their arms.

Kim tried everything—leaning, counting, closing her eyes, and then opening them wide—but nothing worked. She couldn't let herself fall. The team pleaded and encouraged her. They said they had safely caught bigger, heavier people. But Kim would lean back until she came to the crucial point where she had to make a commitment one way or the other, and then she'd straighten up. Eventually, though, with her eyes closed and her body stiff, she broke the point of no return. She committed fully, landed safely—and learned what believers over the centuries have discovered: The life of faith calls for believers to go "all in."

God said, " 'I will be found by you' " (Jeremiah 29:14). He promises that when we begin living His will for our life, we will find it—but only if we never give up. It's risky, because the searching requires a 100 percent commitment. It's not like a diet we try for thirty days and then quit if it doesn't work.

I was invited to travel to Australia to speak at some meetings. On my way out the door of my house the day I was to leave for Australia, I suddenly realized that I didn't have my wallet with me. I searched wholeheartedly, but I couldn't find it anywhere. Now what should I do? I could have called Australia and said, "Sorry. I can't find my wallet; I'll have to cancel the trip." I could have said, "I don't like looking for things. I'd rather miss the trip to Australia than search for my wallet. I'll do something else—something that doesn't require a wallet." No. These alternatives would have been insane. When you've agreed to go to Australia and you've lost your wallet, you search and search and search until you find it.

There are no magic formulas to perseverance—only the simple math of saying, "In order to get what I want, I must keep searching until I find it." And the promise is sure: We'll discover and obtain the great things God has for every believer when we commit fully and continue to do so until we find what we are looking for.

1. Bruce Wilkinson, *The Seven Laws of the Learner* (Sisters, Ore.: Multnomah Publishers, 2005), 85
2. Ellen G. White, *The Great Controversy* (Nampa, Idaho: Pacific Press®, 1950), 525.

Questions for Reflection

1. What has most helped you learn to live God's will for you?

2. This chapter suggests several activities meant to help you engage in God's will. Which one do you think you need to try immediately? Why?

3. To what degree do you think expectations shape people's success in life? Do you know people who expect great things to happen every day? How do their expectations affect what they experience?

4. In what area of your life today do you need to go "all in" with God and fully trust His guiding ways?

5. How have you sensed God's hand guiding you recently? What do you think is His will for your life?

6. If you agree that God's will for us is more about knowing Him than knowing the future, how will your approach to His will change today?

Well Worth the Struggle

While waiting alone in the car for my wife, who was shopping—again—I grabbed a box of cereal from a grocery bag in the back seat, and I began to munch away as I listened to a ball game on the radio. Then some scholarly thoughts that were published on the back of the cereal box caught my eye. Actually, there were very few words on the box. The back panel featured a big picture of the earth and, in the distance, the moon and the stars. The instructions read: "To see the image within the image, fix your eyes on the picture and stare into it until the hidden picture emerges and the other picture fades into the background. For best results, put the center of the picture to your nose and slowly pull the box away." I tried this for about twenty minutes, and I didn't see a thing. I heard some laughing, and, glancing over, I saw a bunch of kids in a minivan parked next to me pointing in my direction.

Ignoring the kids, I continued to stare at the box. Sure enough, after about forty minutes (my wife is a serious shopper), the image within the picture emerged and I saw it—it was a spaceship. The more you take the time to learn how to look at 3-D images, the better you become at it.

Perhaps discovering God's will is also about learning to see—learning to look carefully at and obey what is already before you while patiently waiting for God's plan to emerge. Job said it well after his ordeal with God,

"I know that you can do all things;
    no plan of yours can be thwarted.
[You asked,] 'Who is this that obscures my counsel
      without knowledge?'

Surely I spoke of things I did not understand,
things too wonderful for me to know.

"[You said,] 'Listen now, and I will speak;
I will question you,
and you shall answer me.'
My ears had heard of you
but now my eyes have seen you" (Job 42:2–6).

If anything came to me in the journey of discovering God's will, it was a sense that God isn't hiding His plan for my life. He isn't disguising His will for yours either; there is no game afoot. God has extended His hand for centuries, and many have clasped hands with Him as they walk. But while God isn't playing a game, He does guide by His own rules, and sometimes the ways in which He leads us aren't the ways we would choose. For those of you who have trusted in your own way and want to try His hand instead, God does have a will regarding how He wants us to live.

The way God has led me has been well worth whatever struggle it involved. In *The Desire of Ages*, Ellen White wrote, "God never leads His children otherwise than they would choose to be led, if they could see the end from the beginning, and discern the glory of the purpose which they are fulfilling as co-workers with Him."[1]

Ask any of those people in the sunset of their life who have found God's will and walked step by step with Him if they regret the journey. No, in life we may have many regrets, but those guided by the hand of Christ know that God's will is good. They also know that as long as they walk intimately with Him, His will is being done in them "on earth as it is in heaven." So here is the salient moment of truth on which everything in your life pivots: Do you trust God? Will you follow Him whether or not you understand Him?

Here is my prayer for you: "Lord and Father in heaven, grant to those holding this book that they may find and live Your will. May they sense the peace that comes only from trusting completely in Your guiding ways. Rescue them by Your grace even when the darkness seems to overtake them, and place their feet next to Yours. I pray that as You lead them through life, their journey will testify of Your wisdom, Your power, Your love, and Your plan—Your good and perfect plan. In Christ's name I pray. Amen."

---

1. Ellen G. White, *The Desire of Ages* (Mountain View, Calif.: Pacific Press®, 1940), 224, 225

Go Figure: An Interactive Approach to the Bible

As you consider various approaches to studying the Bible, you will notice that most of the devotional approaches are quite similar. The following is a process that is helpful to me:

1. Look at God's Word . . .

. . . with eyes that are open, observing the details in the text: the words, phrases, names, verbs, emotions, contrasts, lists, conditions. Most of the work of Bible study is detective business—looking for the pieces of the puzzle. You might try underlining, circling, and highlighting specific things you notice, or draw lines to connect ideas in a chapter.

. . . with eyes that imagine, picturing the reality of the event or conversation with your sanctified imagination. (It's OK!)

. . . with eyes that focus, ruminating on one idea, thought, or section at a time.

2. Listen to God's Word . . .

. . . with ears to the world of the biblical characters, so you can understand what the writer meant to say in their time and place.

. . . with ears to your world, so you sense the relevance of God's Word today. The exercise is one of bridge-building!

. . . with ears to recognize the sound of God's voice speaking to your heart and life—personally.

3. Learn from God's Word . . .

. . . with a balanced mind, to measure each passage in light of the whole of Scripture.

. . . with a practical mind, to determine the areas of your life that need renewal and how that might occur.

. . . with a proactive mind that seeks to live differently in light of discovery.

4. Live God's Word . . .

. . . with personal application that directly relates to your circumstances and sphere of influence.

. . . with a pliable heart that is willing to be shaped by your study throughout the day.

. . . with a tangible response to God's Word. (This means a response that's specific, concrete, and measurable. For example: "I'm going to control my temper during the basketball game tonight" [good] versus "I want to control my temper" [inadequate].)

If you found inspiration in this book, you'll also want to read:

Sure Salvation
Philip W. Dunham

"Jesus Loves Me, This I Know, For the Bible Tells Me So."

Kids sing it, why can't we believe it? Sometimes it seems that the badge of membership in the Seventh-day Adventist Church is a gnawing uncertainty about our relationship with Christ and our salvation.

Our salvation is sure *in Christ*. Our Savior is our *only* source of salvation. Author Philip W. Dunham has written this book so you can experience what flawed people throughout Christian history have experienced—the assurance that every believer can and should have—in the "Lamb of God who takes away the sin of the world!" Read *Sure Salvation* and find the peace and joy Christ died to give you.

Paperback, 160 pages.   US$ 13.99
ISBN 13: 978-0-8163-2178-0   ISBN 10: 0-8163-2178-7

Soul Matters
Karl Haffner

Is your life still stuck in "fast forward"? Do you own the twenty-pound, folio-sized, leather-bound, gilded-edged, deluxe Daytimer with the optional wheels? Are you doing more and enjoying it less? Still struggling with soul fatigue? Help is available.

In *Soul Matters,* with humor and wisdom Pastor Karl Haffner points the way to more relief for the "stressed out, worn out, and burned out." In this sequel to *The Cure for Soul Fatigue* (think of it as a second dose of the cure), Karl explores soul questions, soul pain, soul community, and soul goodness. He reminds us all that it is possible to live a sane and balanced life in a world gone mad.

Paperback, 144 pages.   US$12.99
ISBN13: 978-0-1632-2150-6   ISBN 10: 0-8163-2150-7

Order from your ABC by calling **1-800-765-6955**, or get online and shop our virtual store at **<www.AdventistBookCenter.com>**.
- Read a chapter from your favorite book
- Order online
- Sign up for e-mail notices on new products

Prices subject to change without notice.